Reconstructing
the Future

Bauhaus Earth,
Hans Joachim Schellnhuber,
Rocío Armillas Tiseyra (Eds.)

Reconstructing the Future

Cities as Carbon Sinks

BIRKHÄUSER
BASEL

BAUHAUS ● EARTH

contents

foreword

Giovanna Melandri

In June 2022, the whole community working at the MAXXI museum felt a great burst of hope and excitement. It was the museum's 10th anniversary, coinciding with a number of enthusiastic and progressive initiatives. The team from Bauhaus Earth was in Rome for its cohosted conference with the Pontifical Academy of Sciences, Reconstructing the Future for People and Planet. The event brought together an incredible short list of world-size influential speakers, from Francis Kéré to Ursula von der Leyen, including a long list of front-runners in design, planning, the arts, activism, philosophy, and science.

President von der Leyen was in Rome not only to participate in Bauhaus Earth's conference but also to celebrate the first festival of her own project, the New European Bauhaus (NEB), choosing MAXXI as the Italian pivotal venue for a network of synchronous events across Europe. The unusual circumstance of operating such important public events in the immediate aftermath of the COVID-19 vaccine rollout in Europe wasn't a real obstacle for the organizing team, who took inspiration from the constraints of the time to work even harder and make the events program accessible for a broader audience via streaming and digital media.

Our spirits were sky-high at MAXXI, and everybody worked nonstop to prepare for events linked to our anniversary and to the other initiatives. We were happy not only for the opportunity to cross paths with the NEB but also to form a lasting friendship with Bauhaus Earth. The decennial was a good time to look back at our own 10 years' record of exhibitions and projects, and to be proud. And when we reviewed them—from time to time focused on topics such as recycling, energy, science (*Gravity: Imaging the Universe after Einstein*), digital culture (*Low Form: Imaginaries and Visions in the Age of Artificial Intelligence*), food—we felt reassured that we had chosen the right direction for our curatorial agency, and because of that we also felt we were a "natural ally" for the other protagonists of that exciting Roman (early) summer. However, the series of events was not only an opportunity to look back and feel proud of the identity we had built for our museum over a decade of projects and actions. It appeared even more as the right time to discuss and launch our projects for the second decade of MAXXI's life. These projects have to do with the museum's diverse fields of operation: exhibitions and public programs, direct agency in the social and physical space, wider cultural policies. As a backdrop to all this, but certainly not a secondary issue, we felt we were (and are) implicitly participating in a wider, global, and still-open discussion about the mission and identity of contemporary museums in general and museums focusing on the arts in particular.

Concerning our exhibition program, our aim is to keep building on the idea that an art exhibition, and more especially an architecture exhibition, is not only a device for promoting a specific contemporary artist or for displaying a fragment of architectural history. The exhibition, as we felt over these last 10 years of production, is thought of as part of the ongoing construction of an alternative and progressive culture in the fields of art and architecture—a culture that involves alternative design strategies, such as recycling and reuse of spaces and materials, research focus on new and more sustainable building materials, socially aware planning, and integration between arts and science.

On the one hand, we're convinced that we can learn a lot from our past and share this knowledge with the world, considering how the process of building architecture and cities in Italy has always relied on the acknowledgment, reuse, and integration of existing structures. On the other hand, we're conscious of the power an institution like ours wields from its easy access to ideas and proposals from all over the world and from the possibility of sharing and diffusing them to an even larger community of artists, designers, thinkers, and producers. A perfect example of this cognitive-communicative process is the dialogue MAXXI established in this specific frame with NEB and Bauhaus Earth. From Bauhaus Earth, we learn about the potential of new building materials; from NEB, we are reminded how no ethics can be asserted if it does not imply a new aesthetics. The agency of a museum like ours sits right in the middle of this crossroads of ideas, issues, risks, constraints, and new discoveries.

Speaking of the presence of the museum in the physical space of the city of Rome and in the conceptual space of global civilization, MAXXI has taken in the last years a big step toward direct agency. The aim is to materialize in architectural terms the evolution of the museum from a space of preservation and ecstatic contemplation to a space made of research and direct action that looks to the future. To pursue this task, the museum decided to go from MAXXI to "Grande MAXXI" by planning a specific addition where some of the innovative fields of operation will find their home: platforms for the dialogue between technology, science, and art, between the museum and the actual space of the city, between the artists and designers and communities interacting with their proposals. The new building will be neither a simple extension of Zaha Hadid's project, both a masterpiece and a clear product of its time, nor another, competing piece of performative architecture, choosing form and astonishment as its main objective. Chosen via an international competition and designed by a large team led by Ian architecture from Paris and landscape architect Bas Smets from Brussels, the new layout of the museum will be achieved by a large guided intrusion by nature and by an "intelligent box" completing a newly conceived campus for the arts and science of the future. Expanding in the dialogue with the existing structure, the new building will host additional and "displayable" storage space, labs, experimental educational programs, and workshop spaces for innovative coactions involving artists, designers, tech experts, and city planners.

The exciting days of June 2022 were also devoted to the celebration of another aspect of the life of the MAXXI: the new network a museum needs to build around itself. This network has to be the expanded platform for at least two types of action. First, and very new, is the utopia—hopefully a concrete one—of an unprecedented collaboration between bottom-up actions coming from the communities and young activists and the intellectual and political leadership in Europe. Second—close but different—is the idea of the museum as an institution devoted to the creation of an alliance with politics and science on a new basis. This is not the old conflict about local versus global or popular versus elitist, but a common effort based on new assumptions, concerning the future of the planet, the future of communities inhabiting the planet, and the basics of a new dialogue between the political streams, the digital culture, the creative minds, and institutions committed to a negotiation between memory and the future, like us.

To conclude, if most of the network that was spectacularly displayed in the days of June 2022 takes root—Hans Joachim Schellnhuber and Ursula von der Leyen's intuition about the NEB and Bauhaus Earth—everything will come back in a virtuous circle in a field defined by the same values: arts, science, and social engagement as the drivers of a society committed to choosing its own future.

Giovanna Melandri
Rome, February 2023

preface

Hans Joachim Schellnhuber & Rocío Armillas Tiseyra

This book emerges from the Reconstructing the Future for People and Planet conference, held at Casina Pio IV, Vatican City, June 9–10, 2022. As a member of the Pontifical Academy of Sciences (PAS), Hans Joachim Schellnhuber put forward the idea for the conference in 2021. He selected the challenge that currently defines his life's work: to initiate an unprecedented *Bauwende*,[1] to help phase out greenhouse gas emissions in the building sector by 2050, and to contribute to the restoration of the global climate by 2200.

In just three months, we managed to bring together 54 eminent scientists, builders, funders, designers, architects, urban planners, and activists, digitally and in person at the PAS headquarters. We were fortunate that the conference coincided with the first festival of the New European Bauhaus (NEB), a major actor in the rekindled Bauhaus movement. The New European Bauhaus itself surfaced from exchanges between Schellnhuber and President von der Leyen. Indeed, the conference and the festival shared a number of participants, including Francis Kéré, Sheela Patel, Shigeru Ban, and Francesca Bria.

Initially, there was no plan to cover the PAS event with a carefully composed book. However, we realized two things during the planning and execution of the conference: (1) COVID-19 restrictions at the Vatican reduced the number of participants present and able to engage at Casina Pio IV; (2) the questions, agreements, and conflicts, in particular those dealing with inadequacy of current language surrounding the construction of our built environment, should be opened to the critical view of a broader audience. The latter led to our decision to secure an open access license for this publication. We thank MOD21 (ERBUD Group) for the generous sponsorship of this license.

from left to right:
Ursula von der Leyen,
Sheela Patel, Edgar
Pieterse, Hans Joachim
Schellnhuber

Not all those who spoke at the conference in 2022 are represented in this book. It is no easy task, nor even a fair one, to ask authors to render their spoken words into written form. Hearing and reading build different memories. So we ask you, the reader, as best you are able, to hear the words on the following pages, rather than to read them. For it has been a challenge to authors and editors alike to truly convene, in writing, memories made of spoken words.

The 21st century must be the century of *re-entanglement*, where quintessential functions (housing, work, culture, recreation, et cetera) are reintegrated within urban spaces, where socioeconomic and ecological systems form a mutually supportive network of networks (PAS 2022), and where past, present, and future are perceived as interwoven currents in an ocean of time. Our contemporary global system does not serve the future we need to restore our planet. The extraction of resources across geographies is also an extraction over time. Our pursuit of economic growth is our theft from future generations (Monbiot 2021).

Eloquently, Sandrine Dixson-Declève will point to the need to completely uproot our current economic models and measurements. This is a sentiment shared by Marc Palahí, who, echoing Robert F. Kennedy, will note that GDP measures everything except that which is worth measuring at all. Specifically, Klaus Mindrup will give us a glimpse into the absurdities entrenched in contemporary German legislations and institutions, which stall the transition to a system that truly respects our planet. Here, Ursula von der Leyen overlaps, as she speaks to the importance of revolutionizing what is often thought to be the monoliths of the status quo. She highlights the importance of the vibrations in the room[2]—what Ana María Durán Calisto will come to describe as *sumak kawsay* or *el buen vivir*[3]—as the missing element in the policies, legislations, and institutions of

the European Commission designed to implement the European Green Deal. This is how she came to embrace the metaphor of the Staatliche Bauhaus zu Weimar as inspiration for the framework of the New European Bauhaus.

Contributors will detail pathways toward low-impact/no-impact extractive methods for the future construction of our built environment. Elspeth MacRae tells us resistance is already out there, and options for a circular bioeconomy are widespread regardless of their endorsement, or not, by the contemporary extractivist global system. Indeed, Shigeru Ban will share his disappointment with the architectural discipline that led him to explore low-tech construction to shelter those faced with calamity. A sentiment echoed by Xu Tiantian, as she draws our attention to the importance of working with vernacular forms, processes, and materials, with people on the ground, to give meaning and opportunity to the environment we co-inhabit. A vision she sums up in "the rural is global."

In turn, Andreja Kutnar will highlight the importance of an interdisciplinary approach for sustainability and the sensible use of resources. In the vein of cities and technology, Francesca Bria will question the hegemony of either Big Tech or Big State, in favor of Big Democracy as a framework for digital rights. In addition, Carlo Ratti will frame his work within the purpose of Utopia or Oblivion, and details a project on citywide energy storage islands. It will be Wael Al Awar who will disrupt any trending nostalgia for traditional architectures as self-evident pathways to a sustainable future, arguing that local, modern innovation of unlikely place-based materials represents a viable, desirable future. Finally, it will be Sheela Patel who will throw a wrench into our assumptions and question the sole-actor mindset of the architectural discipline in the production of space. She will draw our attention to the fact that the majority of the built environment in the Global South is not in fact developed by developers, designed by architects, or financed by states or firms, but rather by the people themselves, who inhabit it.[4] Which indeed calls for multiple, diverse, and simultaneous actions, rather than a single pathway for all.

from left to right:
Andreja Kutnar, Wael Al Awar, Shigeru Ban

Just as our contemporary system thieves from future generations, so too does it have history. A poignant component in Edgar Pieterse's contribution is when he tells us that conference colleagues spoke "quite a bit of systems thinking, quite a lot of design thinking, a lot of focus on technology, but there is no critical thought about historical path-dependent constraints that shape the power of place-making."[5] In particular, he will question the sinister relationship between ODA[6] and trade relations between the Global North and South, and its impact on, and acceleration of, the climate crisis. This is an argument that will resonate with the process of epistolocide, described by Ana María Durán Calisto as the hegemony of faraway cities (colonial and imperial legacy) preaching a modernity that eradicates all other knowledge systems. Here again Sheela Patel will drive the point home, when she criticizes the exclusion and the excitement of beautiful visuals, which only remind us that there is no clarity in our frameworks on the production of space or on what constitutes inclusion. Just as architects claim to feel accountable to the planet, so too must they feel accountable to one-third of the population that has been excluded for multiple generations.

As one contributor to the book put it, during the editing process, *this is an eclectic project*. Indeed, we hope so, because we believe that the change we need will be defined by the bridges we build between actors and actions.

---

1 German term referring to the necessary paradigm shift in how we build, operate, and demolish the built environment.

2 See page 40.

3 See page 85.

4 See page 193.

5 See page 126.

6 Overseas Development Assistance

References

Monbiot, George. 2021. "Capitalism Is Killing the Planet—It's Time to Stop Buying Into Our Own Destruction." *Guardian*, October 30, 2021.

PAS (Pontifical Academy of Sciences). 2022. "Reconstructing the Future for People and Planet." Final Statement of the Workshop, June 9–10. www.pas.va/en/events/2022/reconstructing_the_future/final_statement.html.

1

bioeconomy: toward sustainable living and biosensitive cities

Joachim von Braun

Bioeconomy to Strategically Transform the Anthropocene

Humankind faces large and growing ecological, social, and economic challenges, which are interlinked in complex ways. The climate crisis has its root cause in the excessive use of fossil fuels and in huge global land use change, both of which have detrimental effects for biodiversity. Energy and land use change relate fundamentally to two sectors, the food sector and the construction sector. Together, these sectors cause almost 70 percent of greenhouse gas emissions (IPCC 2019; IEA 2019). Both sectors need to be guided toward fundamental transformations.

A challenge is that transforming these sectors must have a focus on equity because large parts of the world population depend on these two sectors and have their livelihoods connected to them. More than 500 million small farms form part of the world food systems, many of these farm families live in inadequate housing, and many are among the approximately 830 million undernourished people worldwide (Diao et al., 2023). Employment in the construction sector is estimated to be 8.6 percent of total employment globally (ILO 2021). About 1.1 billion people live in urban slum settlements, and today more than 56 percent of the world's population (4.4 billion inhabitants) live in cities. By mid-century about two-thirds are projected to live in cities (UN DESA 2019).

With the coming urban population boom, a continued massive expansion of construction and food production is expected. In the Anthropocene—the age in which humankind has become an important factor influencing the biosphere, the geosphere, and the atmosphere of the earth—a combination and integration of far-reaching initiatives for more social and technological innovation is necessary. The strategic answer to Anthropocene challenges is an evolution toward a more bio-based economy—a bioeconomy.

The need to reintegrate human economic activity into nature's cycles is widely recognized by now. The challenge of decoupling economic growth from the excessive use of finite resources needs to be tackled. At the same time, shaping the future of work in the digitized, networked world offers opportunities in decentralized setups of urban and rural habitat. Consequently, the very concepts of urban and rural, of cities and villages, may become obsolete in the 21st century.

Evolving Concept of Bioeconomy

Bioeconomy is on the one hand very ancient and traditional (bread baking, beer brewing, food conservation, charcoal production, wood and other plant products, or house and infrastructure constructions) and on the other hand new and innovative (novel biomaterials, biopharmaceuticals, biotechnologically produced ingredients for food, feed, and cosmetics). The innovative bioeconomy is based on scientific and technological progress. It is a central strategic component that can serve the three dimensions of ecological, social, and economic sustainability. Bioeconomy is defined as the "knowledge-based production and use of biological resources, processes and principles to provide products and services in all economic sectors within a sustainable economic system" (IACGB 2020, 14).

Transformation into a post-fossil age would hardly be possible with a closed-loop circular economy alone. A circular-flow economy, with its focus on material flows and recycling routes, is not per se sustainable. It must always ask itself which resource costs and external effects "circulation" (including recycling) actually produces. The bioeconomy goes well beyond the circular-flow economy by focusing on social, ecological, and economic sustainability (El-Chichakli et al. 2016). The bioeconomy takes its model from the cycles of nature and the special abilities of organisms and entire ecosystems. They can reproduce, repair, and adapt to environmental changes. Georgescu-Roegen (1970)—a pioneer of an ecologically oriented economic theory—applied the laws of thermodynamics to economic questions and derived far-reaching consequences for the economic use of nonrenewable resources. Even with recycling—i.e., in recycling management—it is only possible to recover raw materials that have already been used by using energy and materials, and only partially.

In recent years, rapid progress has been made in many areas of the biosciences and life sciences, in particular genomics, which now makes innovations for sustainability possible through digitization and information technology. The life sciences cover research fields as diverse as biology, biochemistry, bioinformatics, biomedicine, biophysics, biotechnology and genetic engineering, nutrition sciences, agricultural sciences, food technology, medicine, medical technology, pharmacy and pharmacology, environmental management, and environmental technology. New knowledge in these areas is of great relevance for bioeconomy and a sustainable society.

In the bioeconomy, the use of biomass comes partly at the expense of forests and may compete with food production on scarce land. These concerns must be taken seriously, because a bioeconomy is not sustainable per se, but must be designed to be sustainable. Ecological sustainability can only be seen in actual improvements in the resource efficiency of the national economy, whereby external effects as well as the so-called rebound effects of changed use and consumption behavior are taken into account. This requires clear concepts for measuring the bioeconomy (Wesseler and von Braun 2017). Bioeconomics must adapt to biomass with limited availability, and must not be misunderstood as a biomass strategy.

Opportunities, Trade-offs, and Synergies in Bioeconomy: Food System in the Bioeconomy

We owe life on earth to a unique cycle in which solar energy is stored in various plants through photosynthesis. Plants are often mentioned in the technical literature as biomass when it comes to their universal function as a renewable and energy-rich carbon carrier. When biomass decomposes, CO_2 and water are produced, which are required for photosynthesis. Around 60 billion tons of biomass (measured in dry matter) is produced annually on land areas such as forests, meadows, steppes, and fields, and a quarter of this growing biomass is already used by humans (Haberl et al. 2007). Most of the plants are used for food, especially animal feed. But fuels and building materials, as well as raw materials for chemicals and industry, also play an important role. In climate mitigation policy, the binding of CO_2 from the atmosphere in forests, agroforests, wetlands, grasslands, and humus soils is of great and increasing importance.

In the area of sustainable food consumption, incentives and product modifications can reduce food waste. Numerous bioeconomic start-ups are working on sustainable alternatives to animal protein. High-protein meat, milk, and egg substitute products are already on the market, and start-ups are in the experimental stage of bringing the synthetic (biotechnical) production of meat from the laboratory to production. In agriculture, rapid success can be achieved in curbing water consumption and overcoming soil degradation. Technological solutions include improved breeding of high-yielding, resistant, and frugal plants. This will be of great importance in view of climate change. Precision agriculture manages to generate new knowledge with the help of automatic data collection and to provide farmers worldwide with information for optimal management. Field robotics is emerging to protect the soil, contain diseases, and dispense with pesticides and herbicides. The catchphrase "urban farming" encompasses various projects for the production of food in large cities, which are to supply the population with fresh vegetables, fruit, and fish.

Biosensitive Cities and Construction

In order to achieve a net-zero carbon building stock by 2050, we need to cut direct building emissions by 50 percent and indirect building emissions by 60 percent by 2030 (IEA 2019). As such, innovative biosensitive solutions are needed in order to reshape the ways we live and consume, reconstruct cities in sustainable ways, and design urban and rural living contexts that function sustainably. This entails new ways to design cities, and new methods of construction with new materials, and all that while providing quality of life for inhabitants. This puts bioeconomy at the center of sustainable reconstruction strategies. By integrating biological principles in urban and rural planning and life, the development of the bioeconomy can contribute to higher levels of quality of life (Global Bioeconomy Summit 2020).

Biobased cities are inspired by nature's design and circulation principles and aim for a high quality of life and a healthy lifestyle for all. In addition to renewable and environmentally friendly building materials, which can even be used in modern high-rise buildings, these concepts deal with closing the material cycles in the city. This concerns the recycling of materials, the extraction of bioenergy from organic waste and wastewater, and the biotechnological recovery of scarce raw materials from wastewater (e.g., phosphorus) and residual materials (e.g., precious metals). The architecture makes use of local conditions and biological knowledge for natural shading, cooling, or heating of buildings and entire districts. Greenery is used strategically for shading, for air purification, to provide a recreation and movement area for the urban population, for the protection of biodiversity, and as a water reservoir and regulator.

The use of biobased and residual materials is a relevant aspect of future architecture and building projects. It should help to minimize the use of energy-intensive and nonrenewable building materials and should also be used for cost-efficient retrofits of existing buildings. In light of their material properties and their improved environmental balance, natural resources can serve as materials for buildings, as general construction materials, or for construction and interior construction. Since humans first began building houses, we have used biological resources such as wood and straw as building materials. In recent years, sustainability and energy efficiency have become increasingly important topics in the construction sector. Innovative and high-tech building materials have been developed from renewable resources. One example is wood fiber insulation materials, but cellulose from defibrated old paper, hemp, flax, meadow grass, straw, and sheep's wool can also serve as raw material for insulation. Urban bioeconomy is not only about construction, but also about urban production. "Green" industrial production and urban farming are becoming relevant. Organic aquaponics and hydroponic greenhouses provide fresh vegetables.

The Way Forward

There is an accelerating global trend into bioeconomy; about 50 countries have newly adopted bioeconomy-related policy strategies in the past decade (Dietz et al. 2018). This trend toward bioeconomy is driven by the need to address resource constraints related to climate, water, energy, and land, by recent advances in microbiology, and by shifts in consumer preferences. New opportunities are arising in bioeconomy for industries, construction, and agriculture, but strategies also need to address conflicting goals with science and policy to ensure innovations for food security and resource protection. Policy for urban and construction transformation should focus on navigating toward sustainable bioeconomy, and fully involving the population. This includes creating strong incentives for innovation to promote sustainability, and encouraging respect and appreciation of nature as the unique inspiration and livelihood of humanity. Accelerated life science and social sciences are fundamental for mobilizing bioeconomy at scale to overcome the Anthropocene's pitfalls (von Braun 2022).

References

Diao, Xinshen, Thomas Reardon, Adam Kennedy, Ruth S. DeFries, Jawoo Koo, Bart Minten, Hiroyuki Takeshima, and Philip Thornton. 2023. "The Future of Small Farms: Innovations for Inclusive Transformation." In *Science and Innovations for Food Systems Transformation*, edited by Joachim von Braun et al., 191–205. Cham, Germany: Springer. https://doi.org/10.1007/978-3-031-15703-5_10.

Dietz, Thomas, Jan Börner, Jan Janosch Förster, and Joachim von Braun. 2018. "Governance of the Bioeconomy: A Global Comparative Study of National Bioeconomy Strategies." *Sustainability* 10: 3190. https://doi:10.3390/su10093190.

El-Chichakli, Beate, Joachim von Braun, Christine Lang, Daniel Barben, and Jim Philp. 2016. "Policy: Five Cornerstones of a Global Bioeconomy." *Nature* 535 (July 14): 221–23. www.nature.com/news/policy-five-cornerstones-of-a-global-bioeconomy-1.20228.

Georgescu-Roegen, Nicholas. 1970. *The Entropy Law and the Economic Process*. Cambridge, MA: Harvard University Press.

Global Bioeconomy Summit. 2020. *Expanding the Sustainable Bioeconomy: Vision and Way Forward*. Communiqué of the Global Bioeconomy Summit 2020, Berlin. gbs2020.net/wp-content/uploads/2020/11/GBS2020_IACGB-Communique.pdf.

Haberl, Helmut, K. Heinz Erb, Fridolin Krausmann, Veronika Gaube, Alberte Bondeau, Christoph Plutzar, Simone Gingrich, Wolfgang Lucht, and Marina Fischer-Kowalski. 2007. "Quantifying and Mapping the Human Appropriation of Net Primary Production in Earth's Terrestrial Ecosystems." *Proceedings of the National Academy of Sciences* 104, no. 31 (July): 12942–47. https://doi.org/10.1073/pnas.0704243104.

IACGB (International Advisory Council on Global Bioeconomy). 2020. *Global Bioeconomy Policy Report (IV): A Decade of Bioeconomy Policy Development around the World*. Berlin: Secretariat of the Global Bioeconomy Summit 2020. gbs2020.net/wp-content/uploads/2021/04/GBS-2020_Global-Bioeconomy-Policy-Report_IV_web-2.pdf.

IEA (International Energy Agency). 2019. *Global Status Report for Buildings and Construction 2019*. Paris: IEA. www.iea.org/reports/global-status-report-for-buildings-and-construction-2019.

ILO (International Labour Organization). 2021. *Impact of COVID-19 on the Construction Sector*. ILO Sectoral Brief. Geneva. www.ilo.org/wcmsp5/groups/public/---ed_dialogue/---sector/documents/briefingnote/wcms_767303.pdf.

IPCC (Intergovernmental Panel on Climate Change). 2019. "Summary for Policymakers." In *Climate Change and Land: An IPCC Special Report on Climate Change, Desertification, Land Degradation, Sustainable Land Management, Food Security, and Greenhouse Gas Fluxes in Terrestrial Ecosystems*, edited by P. R. Shukla et al., 1–36. Cambridge: Cambridge University Press. https://doi.org/10.1017/9781009157988.001.

UN DESA (United Nations, Department of Economic and Social Affairs, Population Division). 2019. *World Urbanization Prospects: The 2018 Revision* (ST/ESA/SER.A/420). New York: United Nations.

von Braun, Joachim. 2022. “Exogenous and Endogenous Drivers of Bioeconomy and Science Diplomacy.” *EFB Bioeconomy Journal* 2 (November): 100029. https://doi.org/10.1016/j.bioeco.2022.100029.

Wesseler, Justus, and Joachim von Braun. 2017. “Measuring the Bioeconomy: Economics and Policies.” *Annual Review of Resource Economics* 9 (October): 275–98. https://doi.org/10.1146/annurev-resource-100516-053701.

2

saving the world by construction

Hans Joachim Schellnhuber

Thank you very much, Madam President, Madam Minister, Ambassadors, Excellencies, ladies, and gentlemen. It is a pleasure to have you all here in this room. The title of my talk may sound a bit pompous: "Saving the World by Construction." However, the built environment is the most important factor in the climate and sustainability equations. Paragraphs 44 and 45 in the encyclical *Laudato si'* from 2015 both cover the importance of the built environment. It is a specific passion of Pope Francis, who was the Archbishop of Buenos Aires and worked in the favelas across the city, so this is near to his heart. I'll read to you a sentence at the end of paragraph 44:

> "We were not meant to be inundated by cement, asphalt, glass, and metal and deprived of physical contact with nature."
> (Encyclical Letter 2015)

As Joachim von Braun already mentioned,[1] the Pontifical Academy of Sciences (PAS) helped to create that encyclical, as did Cardinal Turkson. We had a number of scientific giants involved, and we still have giants in the PAS, including some 25 Nobel laureates. Two members, on whose shoulders we all stand, passed away recently: Mario Molina and Paul Crutzen, dear friends, and preeminent scientists.

I had the privilege to write an obituary for Paul in the *Proceedings of the National Academy of Sciences*, where I also paid tribute to Mario. The motto was *ingeniousness and innocence*, because you learn that these people who know most are also the most humble ones. You probably know that it was Paul J. Crutzen who coined the notion of the Anthropocene, at a meeting in Cuernavaca, Mexico, in spring 2000. Paul submitted the suggestion almost shyly then. And yet the term took flight and created new thinking across disciplines.

After the Second World War, humanity went through a great acceleration, which I recently helped to describe in a paper entitled "The Emergence and Evolution of Earth System Science" (2020). Whatever factor you look at, whatever dimension you inspect, you will see, after 1950, an exponential growth of resource use, material flows, energy conversion, pollution—the list goes on and on (Steffen et al.

2015). This stunning acceleration keeps on creating a completely unsustainable world driven by globalization, which is a rather innocent-sounding notion. However, behind this globalization is all the energetic and material extraction and exponential production and consumption growth, which threaten to break through all planetary boundaries.

Two years ago, a group of scientists from the Weizmann Institute of Science in Israel published a paper that compares living biomass on Earth with anthropogenic mass. The chart shows a steep increase after 1960 of artificial materials such as concrete, aggregates, bricks, asphalt, metals, and plastic. Although everybody talks about plastic now, concrete is the bulk of the anthropogenic mass on our planet. Around two years ago, we experienced a crossover, whereby anthropogenic mass exceeded living biomass on Earth. Prior to the Industrial Revolution, there was an amount of approximately two teratonnes (trillion metric tons of weight) of living biomass; humanity has halved that amount by now. We have killed 1 trillion metric tons of living substance globally and replaced it with man-made matter (Elhacham et al. 2020). This is a deep metabolic transformation of the whole Earth system as reflected by the Anthropocene notion.

Overpopulation is often cited as a major cause of the climate crisis—more people on our finite planet need to use more resources and also pollute more. However, Hickel et al. demonstrate that the biggest share of responsibility lies on the shoulders of the high- and middle-income countries in this regard. The most significant contribution to ecological breakdown comes from the United States of America and, since 1970, the European Union, including the UK, despite Brexit. The rest of the planet, namely the lower- to middle-income countries mostly in the Global South, are contributing almost nothing to overexploiting the climate-relevant capacities of our planet (Hickel et al. 2022). In conclusion, the development status of countries plays an undeniable role here; therefore, it is our legacy and responsibility in Europe and North America to fix this problem.

The climate crisis is the most urgent of all problems, but by far not the only one. For example, the biodiversity crisis is another terrible challenge. Our soils degrade from unsustainable land use and extraction. These are just two of the additional problems to be considered. Let us nevertheless focus on anthropogenic global warming and its impacts now. Together with Rik Leemans, I created the basic structure of Figure 2.1, when we worked on the Third Assessment Report of the Intergovernmental Panel on Climate Change (IPCC); the picture has become widely known as the "burning embers diagram." On the top right side, you see how much global warming (1°, 1.5°, 2°, 3°C, and so on) is required for tipping vital elements of the Earth system, such as melting the Greenland ice sheet and converting the Amazon rain forest into a steppe. In 2001, when we first published this, the red color (indicating tipping certainty) for the Amazon rain forest started at about 6°C warming!

Fig. 2.1 Global and regional risks for increasing levels of global warming

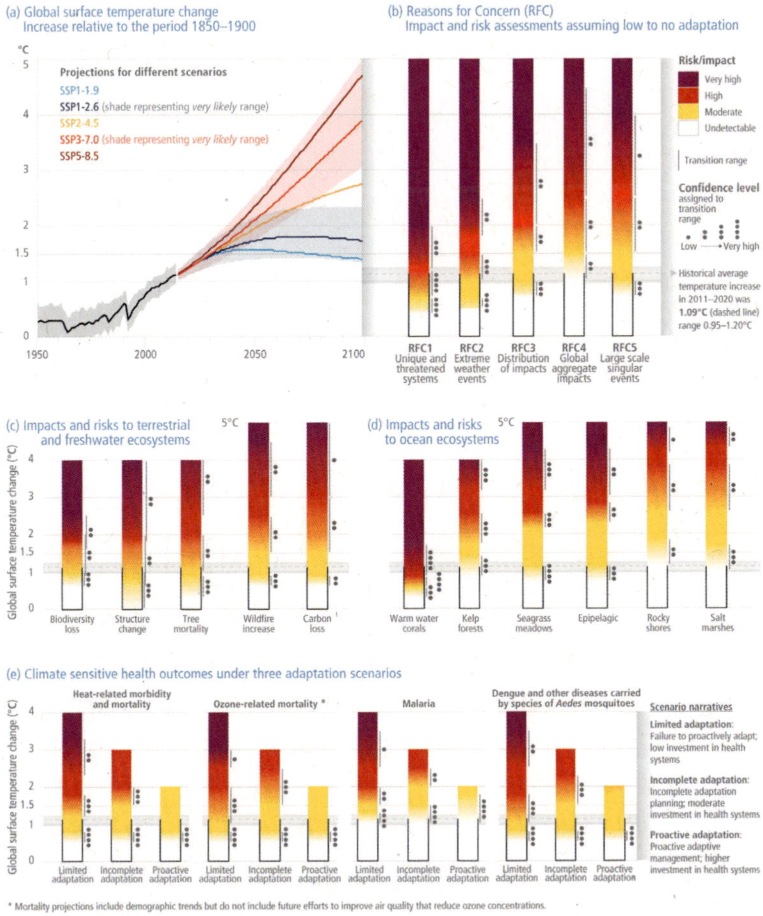

Within 20 years, that red came down to 2°C. We are actually heading for a super-complex disaster now: tipping dynamics in different regions of the planet are likely to conspire and to jointly move us into a hothouse state of the Earth. Thus, for our civilization to persist, it is crucial that we stay below 2°C—but we will not. This is the sad message I have to tell you. We will most probably overshoot global 1.5°C warming, and we will overshoot 2°C as well. As a consequence, the task will be to work the atmosphere one-tenth by one-tenth of a degree back to a safe level for humankind. "Safe" means approximately 1°C above preindustrial levels in our view, i.e., roughly where we are now. *How can it be done?*

There are three necessary conditions for achieving climate restoration. The first one is to reduce global greenhouse gas emissions to zero by 2050. We have Ursula von der Leyen in the room, who initiated and shaped the European Green Deal, which is a major contribution to this international endeavor. However, this is not enough. Secondly, we have to better protect natural ecosystems, for example the Amazon rain forest and large wetlands, which sink a significant percentage of the anthropogenic emission. Without this help from our natural friends, the planet would have warmed already by almost 2°C. Thirdly, we have to create additional carbon sinks that remove a huge portion of the CO_2 that has accumulated in the atmosphere since the Industrial Revolution.

This deliberate extraction of carbon from the air is a novel challenge, which requires unprecedented approaches. The recent IPCC report *Global Warming of 1.5°C* (IPCC 2018) estimated that a tremendous amount of "negative emissions" would have to come from bioenergy, accompanied by carbon capture and storage. In my view, this will not do the job, since it would mean establishing an entirely new worldwide infrastructure, which would cost prohibitive amounts of time and money. Instead of this artificial scheme, there is a more natural and efficient way toward negative emissions, if we turn to the built environment.

I often refer to the latter as *the elephant in the climate room*. We might call it the white elephant or the gray elephant or the black elephant,

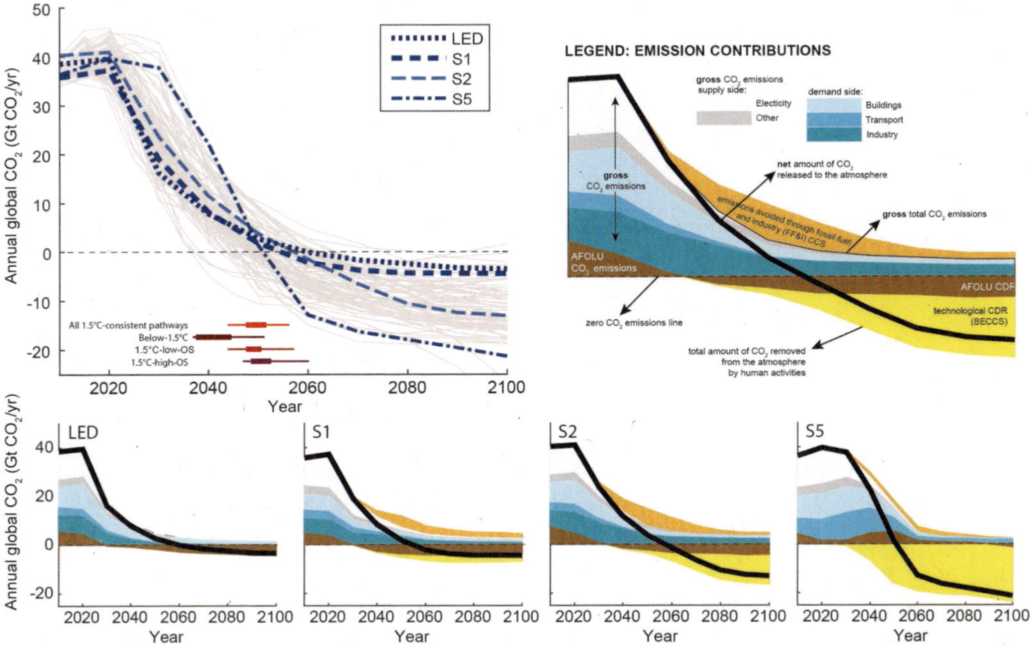

Fig. 2.2 Evolution and breakdown of global anthropogenic CO_2 emissions up to 2100

but it is still an elephant. Why? Because approximately 40 percent of global greenhouse gas emissions derive from the built environment, through the development of buildings and infrastructures, through their operation, and through their demolition (IEA 2019). At present in the EU, the built environment accounts for one-third of the overall waste created (Communication Unit 2022). Therefore, this part of our technical civilization is the most important factor in the sustainability equation. Nevertheless, everybody talks, for instance, about aviation, which accounts for only about 2 percent of global emissions (Ritchie 2020).

However, the 40 percent figure is not a solid finding; some scholars have recently argued that even more than 50 percent of worldwide CO_2 emissions emerge from the built environment (Weidner et al. 2021). We actually need more sophisticated and detailed analyses over the total life cycle of buildings and settlements. I am calling on the pertinent science to weigh in here.

Let us start talking about negative emissions now. They can be realized at appropriate scale and reasonable cost if we *reforest the*

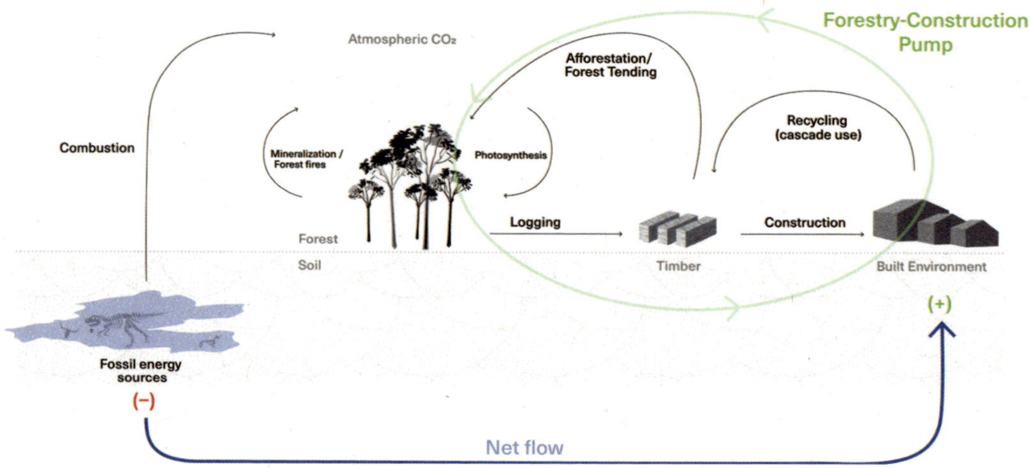

Fig. 2.3
The Forestry-Construction Pump

planet and retimber the city. Bastin et al. (2019) started an important discussion on the global tree restoration potential. Although the exact number of hectares and the locations are still discussed by experts, we have a huge area (possibly 1 billion hectares) of degraded land on this planet, which we could turn into vital ecosystems again, managed forests, and other managed carbon sinks.

Galina Churkina and I, and other close colleagues, published a paper in 2020 about buildings as a global carbon sink, where we calculated that we could take a lot of the historic emissions out of the atmosphere by turning to organic architecture (Churkina et al. 2020).

Figure 2.3 illustrates the Forestry-Construction Pump, a concept that combines sustainable forestry and regenerative construction in order to remove large amounts of CO_2 from the atmosphere and restore preindustrial climate conditions on this planet in the long run (two centuries). The scheme involves a number of processes and steps: reforestation of degraded land; appropriate harvesting of biomass; replanting of trees in order to maintain productive and resilient forests; construction of buildings and infrastructures with wood and bamboo; recycling of organic materials within the built environment; and so on. Together, the respective schemes and cycles involved create a super-loop that pumps out the CO_2 that has accumulated in the atmosphere as a result of historic emissions. This approach takes advantage of the natural properties of plants to convert our pollution through photosynthesis into precious raw materials for construction. Note that the more carbon the air contains, the better this process works (CO_2 fertilization effect). At the same time, we benefit from the amazing progress made over the last decades in using timber, bamboo, and derived materials in architecture and design at all scales.

I will now share with you a few numbers on that, because I did a back-of-the-envelope calculation on climate restoration. At the beginning of the Industrial Revolution, the atmospheric CO_2 concentration was about 280 parts per million (ppm) (Ganopolski 2016). This year, we approached 420 ppm, so we have added some 140 ppm.[2] In terms of weight, this is 1 trillion tons of CO_2, corresponding to an increase of 50 percent compared with the original level. We could take out these 140 ppm if we first plant and foster 500 billion trees, i.e., approximately 50 trees for every human being. This represents a one-time cost of around €500 per person. Secondly, we need to harvest enough biomass from existing forests, new forests, and plantations to build 2 billion homes from timber, bamboo, et cetera during the course of the 21st century. This would take us back to the preindustrial CO_2 concentration of 280 ppm.

Now, if we are not fully successful with this approach and only manage to plant half of the 500 billion trees, we could still subtract 70 ppm from 420 ppm. Thereby, we would come up with 350 ppm, which scientists consider to be a safe operating level for humanity (Rockström et al. 2009). You see, the Forestry-Construction Pump can become a crucial element in the global climate equation!

In a way, this bold yet nature-based scheme would replay the game nature itself played some 300 billion years ago, in the Carboniferous period. During this geological age, vegetation was lush, CO_2 levels were higher, and the climate was warmer and wetter than today. At that time, most of the currently exploited fossil fuel resources (particularly hard coal) were created. It all started with the transformation of dead biomass in wetlands, via geochemical processes under anoxic conditions. Back then, the abundant vegetation extracted a gigantic amount of CO_2 from the atmosphere, and if that removal had gone on for another 20 or 50 million years, our planet would have been pushed into a "Snowball Earth" state again: an almost complete glaciation of the globe (Feulner 2017). It would have been the opposite of a "Hothouse Earth" state, which we may be heading for now. If that had happened, we would not be sitting here today in the Casino Pio IV. Nature did a fantastic job of extracting CO_2 from the atmosphere then. In the course of this (and perhaps also the next) century, we should deliberately replay this planetary process by turning cities and their infrastructures into processed organic mass.

Currently, there are already a number of initiatives under the Bauhaus Earth umbrella, which we created in Germany in 2019. These initiatives codevelop with the New European Bauhaus as announced by the President of the European Union in her State of the Union speech in 2020 (von der Leyen 2020).

Why is the Bauhaus a good metaphor for the new take on the built environment? Well, the key notion here is Gesamtkunstwerk, a German loanword referring to a work of art that makes use of all or many art forms—or at least strives to do so. In the context of the built environment, the word invokes the purposeful composition of all available capacities: knowledge, science, architecture, design, urban planning, art. In essence, it calls for a holistic solution to a problem.

What was the problem at that time, in 1919, after the destruction of the First World War? It was to provide decent accommodations and livable spaces—not just for the elite, but for ordinary people. The Staatliche Bauhaus zu Weimar turned to serial production, prefabrication, and all those schemes exploiting the industrial opportunities of that time. Today, the challenge is even bigger. We have a larger population and multiple crises to handle. We need a truly holistic approach, but we need to think of the Bauhaus in completely different terms in the 21st century, and not just because of the accelerating climate crisis. Allow me a *Gedankenexperiment* (thought experiment) and ask: *What if CO_2 were not a greenhouse gas and there was no anthropogenic global warming? Would the built environment be sustainable? Would it be inclusive? Would it be beautiful?* The evident answer is: not at all!

Even if the climate challenge did not exist, we would have to render our cities, which are defining entities of every civilization and culture, much more inclusive and beautiful than they are today. Ursula von der Leyen keeps on emphasizing this when she talks about the New European Bauhaus. The built environment is vital when we look at the history of humankind. Cities, even megacities, have existed for thousands of years and are deeply entangled with social evolution. Therefore, regardless of the contemporary environmental crises, we have to redesign the built environment for a better future. If we are not able to do this, everything will be lost. Yet being successful here is the precondition for creating a *good Anthropocene*, in which many coming generations can thrive.

The term *Anthropocene* often—too often—carries a negative connotation. Yes, humankind has become a geological force on Earth and we are about to destroy our own livelihoods. But this is not fate; it is an error of a development trajectory that can be corrected! In essence, this correction means switching from a dumb linear petro-economy to a *smart circular bioeconomy* (Stahel 2016). If we embrace the latter, the evidently sustainable one, then most capital stocks on this planet will get dramatically de/revaluated. Qatar and Iran, for example, share the biggest gas field in the world (Reuters 2010). This capital would be annihilated, since the use of fossil gas would not take place anymore and therefore would not yield profit. The gas field would simply turn into a stranded asset. The Democratic Republic of Congo, by contrast, would become one of the biggest capital holders in the world, the "Saudi Arabia of the bioeconomic age": it is a huge country with abundant natural resources supported by a tropical climate.

My final remarks are the following: I wasted some years of my scientific youth working on the foundations of quantum mechanics; later I focused on complex systems and network theory. If you combine the two fields cleverly, you eventually arrive at artificial intelligence emerging from quantum computing. What we still call "digitalization" will experience a great acceleration and become the most powerful cognitive tool on earth (Musser 2018). Everything we dream about computing powers will be changed and transformed.

This provides you with a metaphor for the potential two sides of the future's coin: On one side, we will have unprecedented high-tech capacities created by scientific and operational ingenuity. On the flip side, we have to preserve the biosphere of our planet, which is not only securing the living conditions for humankind but also offers a cornucopia of amazing evolutionary solutions to problems of all types. This way, *we bring together high-tech and no-tech*. I argue that the next phase of the Anthropocene may be the "Cyborganic Age," where utterly advanced computing and processing is mixed harmoniously with nature-based schemes.

The built environment, the villages and cities of the future, is the prime place where evolution can dovetail with civilization, where natural and technical systems merge and complement each other again, at an unprecedented level of formal beauty and functional excellence. We have tried to capture this in the Bauhaus Earth Charter *Toward Re-entanglement*.[3]

Thank you very much for your kind attention.

---

1 Joachim von Braun contributed a written chapter to this book. Hans Joachim Schellnhuber is referring to his oral contribution at the Reconstructing the Future for People and Planet conference, on June 9, 2022; see www.youtube.com/watch?v=HEKjlJxz6Qw&list=PLPHLdH2gKE0ccf5t6ili9U_rZwRQ2lkBB.

2 https://gml.noaa.gov/ccgg/trends/monthly.html

3 Can be accessed at www.bauhauserde.org.

References

Bastin, J.F., Y. Finegold, C. Garcia, D. Mollicone, M. Rezende, D. Routh, C.M. Zohner, and T.W. Crowther. 2019. "The Global Tree Restoration Potential." *Science* 365, no. 6448: 76–79.

Churkina, Galina, Alan Organschi, Christopher P.O. Reyer, Andrew Ruff, Kira Vinke, Zhu Liu, Barbara K. Reck, T.E. Graedel, and Hans Joachim Schellnhuber. 2020. "Buildings as a Global Carbon Sink." *Nature Sustainability* 3, no. 4: 269–76. https://doi.org/10.1038/s41893-019-0462-4.

Elhacham, E., L. Ben-Uri, J. Grozovski, Y.M. Bar-On, and R. Milo. 2020. "Global Human-Made Mass Exceeds All Living Biomass." *Nature* 588, no. 7838: 442–44.

Encyclical Letter. 2015. *Laudato Si' of the Holy Father Francis on Care for Our Common Home*. Vatican City: Vatican Press. www.vatican.va/content/dam/francesco/pdf/encyclicals/documents/papa-francesco_20150524_enciclica-laudato-si_en.pdf.

Feulner, G. 2017. "Formation of Most of Our Coal Brought Earth Close to Global Glaciation." *Proceedings of the National Academy of Sciences* 114, no. 43: 11333–37.

Hickel, Jason, Daniel W. O'Neill, Andrew L. Fanning, and Huzaifa Zoomkawala. 2022. "National Responsibility for Ecological Breakdown: A Fair-Shares Assessment of Resource Use, 1970–2017." *Lancet Planetary Health* 6: 342–49. https://doi.org/10.1016/S2542-5196(22)00044-4.

Ganopolski, Andrey, Ricarda Winkelmann, and Hans Joachim Schellnhuber. 2016. "Critical Insolation—CO_2 Relation for Diagnosing Past and Future Glacial Inception." *Nature* 529: 200–203. https://doi.org/10.1038/nature16494.

IEA. 2019. *Global Status Report for Buildings and Construction 2019*. Paris: IEA. www.iea.org/reports/global-status-report-for-buildings-and-construction-2019.

IPCC (International Panel on Climate Change). 2018. *Global Warming of 1.5°C: An IPCC Special Report on the Impacts of Global Warming of 1.5°C above Pre-industrial Levels and Related Global Greenhouse Gas Emission Pathways, in the Context of Strengthening the Global Response to the Threat of Climate Change, Sustainable Development, and Efforts to Eradicate Poverty*. Edited by Valérie Masson-Delmotte et al. Geneva: IPCC. www.ipcc.ch/site/assets/uploads/sites/2/2019/06/SR15_Full_Report_High_Res.pdf.

Musser, George. 2018. "Job One for Quantum Computers: Boost Artificial Intelligence." *Quanta Magazine*, January 29, 2018. www.quantamagazine.org/job-one-for-quantum-computers-boost-artificial-intelligence-20180129/.

Reuters. 2010. "Factbox: Qatar, Iran Share World's Biggest Gas Field." Editor's Picks. July 26, 2010. www.reuters.com/article/us-northfield-qatar-idUSTRE66P1VV20100726.

Ritchie, Hannah. 2020. "Sector by Sector: Where Do Global Greenhouse Gas Emissions Come From?" *Our World in Data*, September 18, 2020. https://ourworldindata.org/ghg-emissions-by-sector.

Rockström, Johan, Will Steffen, Kevin Noone, Åsa Persson, F. Stuart Chapin III, Eric F. Lambin, Timothy M. Lenton, et al. 2009. "A Safe Operating Space for Humanity." *Nature* 461, no. 7263: 472–75. www.nature.com/articles/461472a.

Science Communication Unit, ed. 2022. "Science for Environment Policy." European Commission DG Environment News Alert Service. Bristol, England: University of the West of England. Accessed January 2023.

Stahel, W.R. 2016. "Circular Economy." Comment Section. *Nature* 531: 435–38.

Steffen, Will, Wendy Broadgate, Lisa Deutsch, Owen Gaffney, and Cornelia Ludwig. 2015. "The Trajectory of the Anthropocene: The Great Acceleration." *Anthropocene Review* 2, no. 1: 81–98. https://journals.sagepub.com/doi.org/10.1177/2053019614564785.

Steffen, Will, Katherine Richardson, Johan Rockström, Hans Joachim Schellnhuber, Opha Pauline Dube, Sébastien Dutreuil, Timothy M. Lenton, and Jane Lubchenco. 2020. "The Emergence and Evolution of Earth System Science." *Nature Reviews Earth & Environment* 1: 54–63. https://doi.org/10.1038/s43017-019-0005-6.

von der Leyen, Ursula. 2020. "Building the World We Want to Live In: A Union of Vitality in a World of Fragility." State of the Union Address by President von der Leyen at the European Parliament Plenary. Brussels, September 16, 2020.

Weidner, Stefanie, Alexandra Mrzigod, Roland Bechmann, and Werner Sobek. 2021. "Graue Emissionen im Bauwesen—Bestandsaufnahme und Optimierungsstrategien." *Beton- und Stahlbetonbau* 116, H. 12: 969–77. https//doi.org/10.1002/best.202100065.

3

the new european bauhaus vision

Ursula von der Leyen

Thank you very much for inviting me to this exciting meeting with these distinguished guests, outstanding in their profession. John Schellnhuber,[1] it is the perfect match that I can mirror the impressive presentation you just gave, from the side of politics. I have been thinking a lot in preparation for this meeting, how to create a common ground for all of us. I think the common ground that we have is that we all know in this room, and those who meet us virtually, that creation was entrusted to us, but we do not own it. It does not belong to us, and our responsibility is to preserve it, to improve it, if possible, but most of all to hand it over to the next generation, to our children and grandchildren. We also know that for far too long we have forgotten about this responsibility.

We built, we destroyed, we polluted, we wasted or we are wasting, we extract. Indeed, what we need is a completely new model of reducing, consuming, engineering, and growing and creating prosperity for the world, but in a different way, in a way that we do not take away anymore from nature, but one in which we give back. This is something which, before I came into office, was very clear to me, and one of the key figures to give me the conviction that this is the right way to go was actually John Schellnhuber, who at that time gave incredibly impressive presentations in the ministry I was leading on global security and climate change, and the devastation of what our actions on the environment do to populations and the conflicts that evolved from these actions.

I was deeply convinced that there needed to be one big priority, and, today, that is the European Green Deal. At present, with the European Green Deal we have, all 27 member states agreed on two goals: to be climate neutral by 2050, and to reduce greenhouse gas emissions by at least 55 percent by 2030. This is now enshrined in law. This is the European climate law, so it is not only a vision or goal, it is the law. Now we have the task of putting that law on track for implementation. We have produced a whole range of legal acts in different sectors. We look at the energy sector, oil, gas, coal, and, on the other hand, renewables. We are looking at the industrial processes, mobility, agriculture, and housing. As we heard, around 40 percent of the greenhouse gas emissions come from the built environment.[2]

In Europe, we put €53 billion into Next Generation, this is only devoted to renovation.

At that point when we designed all these strategies, all these legal proposals, we looked at science; we have all these impact assessments, we have the evidence, the scientific bodies. Yet, after a year or a year and a half, I felt something was missing. It was very hard for me to put it into words, this feeling that something was missing. Basically, the soul is missing or the heart is missing, the emotion is missing. Of course, science is so incredibly important, facts and figures, and it has to be evidence-based and the legal proposals have to be proper. All this is correct. Yet the heart and the soul for this huge transformation we have to undergo, taking people along, was missing.

For example, after 100 days in office, the pandemic hit and I was aware that the loss of biodiversity is one of the fertile grounds and the driving factor of this pandemic. We saw from one point to the next that something fundamental had to change. What was missing in this big transformation machinery, let me put it this way, was the view of the individual, the individual person in their dignity, and how it fits the machinery I have just described.

There is the recognition within the individual that it matters in what environment you are in. It matters what you see. It matters what you hear. It matters what you feel. What you touch. My children would say it is the vibrations in the room that matter. The missing that I expressed earlier became the understanding that we need more than the political framework. We need a grassroots movement that is coming from the individual point of view and dealing with this whole topic, not as a top-down but as a bottom-up movement.

This was the beginning of the idea that we need a New European Bauhaus, because as John Schellnhuber just described, the Bauhaus also initially accompanied the transformation of industrialization. Thinking about it from the individual point of view and the built environment, here it is the transformation toward a green sustainable way to live and to produce and to consume, accompanied by all the forces that are necessary to have a bottom-up movement to fill it with life. How did we start with a New European Bauhaus?

We started with calling for the grassroots movement in a co-creation phase; the first six months were dedicated to listening to what was coming in. Not that we designed the New European Bauhaus top down, but we listened to the world—not only to Europe, but to the world. It was overwhelming the input that came from all over the world, which showed us there already is something that is the answer to the New European Bauhaus, but it has to be channeled. It has to be put in a form, it has to be brought together. It has to find a platform to develop. Hundreds of experts were joining or were commenting, were bringing in their ideas, their initiatives. We started a co-creation period with millions of discussions, and we saw, almost two years later, how broad the grassroots movement already was, how much is out there to come along with the New European Bauhaus.

The New European Bauhaus is looking at a different way to deal with our built environment. We have, for example, initiatives that are developing concepts for schools. How are schools to be built in a New European Bauhaus atmosphere or production process? Architecture—you are the experts here in the room for this topic—how to make it more sustainable and better for pupils and teachers. In the Czech Republic, citizens and architects, for example, were working on concepts on how to transform their whole city into a better place to live. On Saturday, in two days' time, we will award the New European Bauhaus Prize. We received thousands of applications. It was so much that it was really a challenge to choose. All of them are winners, but it shows what is out there already. We have created the New European Bauhaus lab, to give a space for co-creation for the projects that are coming in, to develop them in the sense of the New European Bauhaus. And the New European Bauhaus is spreading. We have, for example, the Bauhaus of the Mountains that is led by a northern Italian Tyrol Initiative. We have the Nordic Bauhaus that is focused around circularity and low-carbon architecture. There is the Bauhaus of the Danube, which brings together all the countries that are located along this wonderful river.

We have two main pillars besides the topic of participation. The first one is sustainability, of course. The New European Bauhaus works basically like an incubator for all the initiatives and plans that are out there, and this longing, from a wide share of citizens, to be part of this transformation toward sustainability and the Green Deal—I would not say the European Green Deal, but the global Green Deal that we basically need—and to bring in their knowledge, and their profession, and their expertise. We are now building a New European research center in Seville, which will host around 400 international scientists. This building will not only be fully carbon neutral, but energy positive. A building that is not only not taking more from nature than it gives back, but is giving back more than it takes from nature, which is, in very practical terms, sharing renewable energy that it produces with the general grid.

The New European Bauhaus has another ambition besides sustainability and participation, and that is—I would perhaps call it beauty or quality of life. We all know, and I do not have to tell you, what the built environment, the room we are discussing in here, what an influence it has on us. By now, the idea of the New European Bauhaus, for example, has reached the fashion industry, which is connected with an enormous number of problems. I am just speaking about resource use, waste, and chemicals, to name a few. Therefore, the movement is to develop fashion in a different way, in a sustainable way, in the principles of the New European Bauhaus, and to be associated with the idea of beauty, of aesthetics, of quality of life, in a sustainable way, in a nature-protective way, in a climate-friendly way.

A project in Luxembourg just won the New European Bauhaus Prize for building a day care center and a primary school completely from wood, and only with materials such as straw, clay, or wool, and the effect it has on teachers and pupils and children in this day care center and in this school. I like the idea you cited, John Schellnhuber, from Pope Francis. I had chosen this one too, it shows how much beauty resonates in us. He said that humans are not meant to be inundated by cement and steel, but building more with natural elements like wood, which is good both for the planet and for the well-being of people.

Since starting the New European Bauhaus initiative, we have more than 450 partners worldwide joining us, from diverse sectors, professions, sectors, and crafts. Artists of different dimensions who say what you are doing resonates with me, let me join and bring in my expertise, my niche knowledge, my enthusiasm and passion. Later today, we will kick off the New European Bauhaus Festival at the MAXXI Museum. It will have more than 200 events that will take place all over Europe and more than 100 projects displayed in Brussels alone. It shows how much is out there already.

I want to finish this short introduction with one thought that shows the dimension of the New European Bauhaus, and that is Ukraine. The destruction of this horrible and atrocious war in Ukraine—there are almost no words for it. We will start to reconstruct Ukraine, and this is not only in our European interest, I think it is our moral duty to give a strong contribution in this reconstruction of Ukraine. Of course, the whole world has to help. The international financial institutions will have to help, but we have a moral duty and responsibility to reconstruct Ukraine. I have spoken a lot with President Zelensky about how to address it. We are creating a platform to channel all these different initiatives for the funding and the ideas for a Marshall Plan for Ukraine. Most importantly, and if you think of the inner images you have right now when I speak about Ukraine, it is these wounded and scarred houses from all the shelling and bombing, the rubble, the destruction that we see in our inner pictures.

We will reconstruct Ukraine, but we should do it in a better and in a different way. I am responsible for the money; we will be responsible together for the reforms linked to the investment in that country. It will be led and owned by Ukraine—they decide how to reconstruct their country—but they are already asking for training projects so that the way we reconstruct Ukraine is leapfrogging into a sustainable future, not falling back into the old structures and patterns, but leapfrogging forward, with the principles of the New European Bauhaus. If we invest these billions and billions in the reconstruction, if we link it with reforms—which, by the way, will pave the way for entry in the European Union—then we should do it in a way as best we can, and this is with the principles of the new European budget.

We need a lot of input from you. It is wonderful and inspiring that you have this conference on Reconstructing the Future for People and Planet today.

Many thanks for having me. And we need you. Thank you.

---

1 Ursula von der Leyen is referring to Hans Joachim Schellnhuber.

2 See page 31.

4

critical appraisal of wood as a building material

Andreja Kutnar

A pleasure to be here with you today. I titled my presentation "Critical Appraisal of Wood as a Building Material" because I am a wood scientist. In the last few years I've been following how we are developing, and at the same time wanted to make sure that we do not forget the past and the knowledge that was there before. I come from Slovenia, from the University of Primorska and research institute InnoRenew. At the same time, I am an active member of Wood for Bauhaus Alliance, created when the New European Bauhaus was established. We want it to be heard around Europe and beyond that we can support the development of the building environment.

To start, I will ask you: Where would you rather be, in the upper photo or the lower one [Figure 4.1]? Each of you can answer in your mind. I will tell you. You would like to be in the lower one because people come from nature and that is the environment we are comfortable in.

The fact is that many of us are spending 80 to 90 percent of our time indoors (USGBC 2011). The same question again: In which photo would you rather be, right or left [Figure 4.2]? Again, I would say most likely in the left one because it is built of natural material, wood.

Regenerative sustainability is an expression that, currently, is not used enough when we are tackling climate change and when we discuss how we want to preserve our planet. It is not only about reducing the environmental harm, but about creating a positive impact. We need to go toward regeneration. When doing this in the built envi-

Fig. 4.1 Outdoor environment

Fig. 4.2 Indoor environment

ronment, we want to transform it into a carbon sink. We should not forget that we need to include new buildings as well as the building stock that already exists. It is my belief that timber is the material that can be used for both.

It is an ideal material for so-called restorative environmental and ergonomic design, where we are not only achieving the sustainability objectives and goals, but we are also connecting humans to nature. A natural material like wood is a very important way to connect people to nature while indoors. It has many impacts on us. It can provide health benefits and also, when we connect people to nature, it causes them to care about the environment (Burnard and Kutnar 2015).

Wood as a material is a very complex result of nature. We can go from the forest to the trees to the boards, which we can see, but there is so much in the micro- and nanostructure of it. With a good understanding and knowledge about the materials on these different levels, we can construct, I would say, the built environment of the future.

In the beginning of my presentation, I mentioned the past, and here I would like to share with you an example of how, many years ago, the industry was directing the cultivation of forests and the trees for specific parts of the Venetian navy needs. Today, we do not do this anymore, but we have knowledge about the material on different levels.

We could say we are going into the sky. We construct higher buildings every year. It is not my intention to say we need to go high, but my intention is to share with you that we are capable of making cities and other new urban regions with timber.

Why is wood so important? It has already been emphasized today a few times. One aspect of it is that true circularity can be achieved. Renewable materials can be used in circles, and with proper management of the forest we do not take anything from nature.

Today we often see, at waste collection facilities, that when wood comes to the end of its life cycle, it is used for energy. I would say we should avoid this. Let us encourage one another not to burn wood. What we should do is use it in a cascade way, going from the boards in large dimensions, in the next cycle going down to the fibers, making engineered wood products out of it. And only at the end of multiple life cycles is when we can use it for energy.

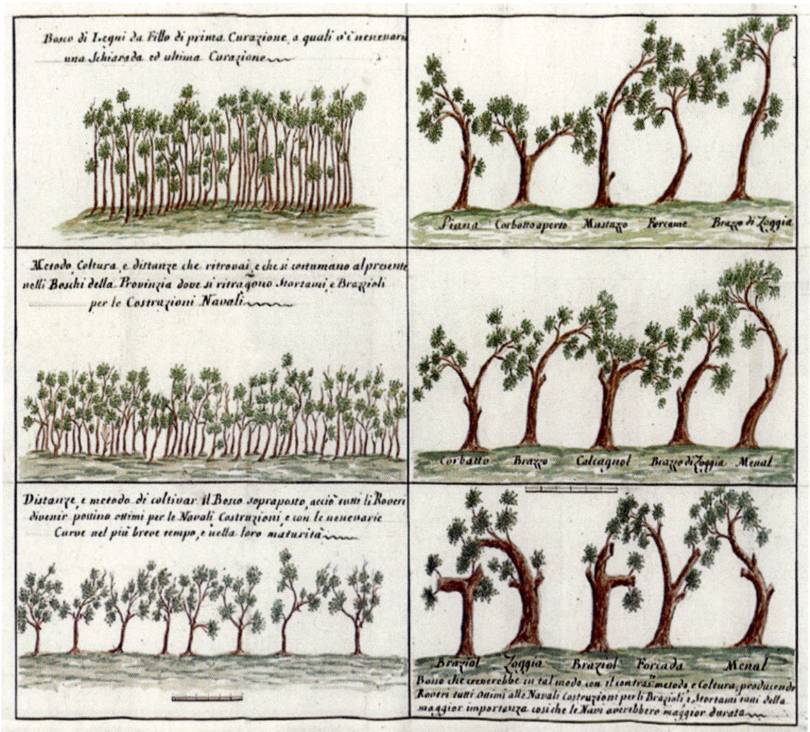

Fig. 4.3 Illustration of oak forest cultivation and various forms of pruning for needs of the Venetian navy

We often discuss which is the appropriate material for different purposes. The fact is that we need to have the appropriate choice of materials for the appropriate use. For example, it is the carbon stock in wood-based materials that is the reason we need to go toward cascading use of wood.

I would say *we need to use more wood*. I hope that there are many of you around who agree with me. How do we do this? My strong belief is that an interdisciplinary approach and modern research fields need to be combined with the sustainability and sensible use of natural resources—in the case of my presentation today, wood. We need to be applying modern technologies. Virtual reality can be one of them. We should include people in the designs and show them, before they make a decision about where they want to live, what their home will look like.

We should not forget that the planet is changing. The new timber species that should be used in the built environment are among us. By knowing wood as a material, we can modify it and achieve the needed properties for certain applications. We can turn poplar, a fast-growing plantation wood, into construction material. I could go on and on, but I think it is very important to come back to the built environment and humans. Restorative, environmental, and ergonomic design is bringing the person back into the center, looking at how the built environment is affecting us; and, as was emphasized today, we should be using local materials. I believe in Europe we have enough wood that we can use for construction (Nabuurs et al. 2018). Design for disassembly is something that will enable us, after the first cycle of a building, to reuse timber, the engineered wood product, in a new way and a new built environment.

It is important that by building these buildings we are connecting people with nature. One way is with the material, but we should not forget also natural light and sounds of nature. I could go further on this. At the same time, we need to be aware that constructing with timber also requires that we be very careful and use timber properly. We still need to learn, and therefore we need demonstrations. We need to monitor, apply modern technologies to monitor the perfor-

Fig. 4.4 Koper's Servite Monastery[1] courtyard view, Slovenia

mance of buildings. Monitoring of buildings can tell us when the building needs to be refurbished and needs to be repaired, as well as how it is behaving in different climates.

There is a project that is currently under way in France: a demonstration building. It is not my intention to go into detail about this demonstration, but I want to encourage everyone: let's make demonstrations and let's educate one another.

Going back to what I mentioned at the beginning, it is not only about new buildings, it also needs to be about the old building stock, especially in Europe, that we need to decarbonize. Figure 4.4 and Figure 4.5 show Koper's Servite Monastery, which we are currently renovating. I allowed myself to bring a few brochures that are outside the room and you're welcome to take them. There is a treasure of knowledge from the past in this building that, with the modern technologies, we can record, and we can pass on to new generations.

For the end of this presentation, I will walk you through the nine Rs, the circular economy concept, and how timber can be placed in this concept of nine Rs.

Fig. 4.5 Koper's Servite Monastery ceiling renovation, Slovenia

1. Refuse: We should not always want more and more. Sometimes we need to make the decision that certain materials are not appropriate.
2. Rethink: Why not make products that are currently made from other materials? For example, wooden tiles or radiator grids produced out of wood. We can modify wood and achieve performance required in different applications.
3. Reduce: When we are constructing, for example, there is waste, also wood. Let us reduce it, and whatever waste is created, let's reuse it.
4. Reuse it for a certain purpose.
5. Repair: Sometimes we go toward the easy path, but it is important that we also go toward repairing, taking up the challenges with the purpose of creating the built environment together and for our improved well-being.
6. Refurbishing: Let us connect with the local societies and create together, as the New European Bauhaus says, another environment in which to live. These are my colleagues, my researchers from InnoRenew, who refurbished the benches in Izola town.
7. Remanufacture: In cascade use, waste wood, for example, can be used in particleboards.
8. Repurpose: We can always find another use for the material that we are using.
9. Recycle: Again, I could go into the engineered wood products where fibers are being used; we do not need to just burn the wood.

In the end, we should not forget all the other renewables that exist. As stated, I wanted to focus on wood, but at the same time I want to emphasize it is not only wood that is important. There are also other renewable materials we should use in the built environment.

My belief is that the next step should be to accelerate knowledge transfer to co-create a beautiful and sustainable built environment for all. InnoRenew Beyond is what we call this project at our institute. We want to learn how to transfer all the knowledge that we have at the institute from scientists who are discovering new knowledge to the society and economy. We are not the only ones. Many research institutions and universities exist around the world. We need to connect their scientific knowledge and accelerate its transfer into the real world.

Thank you very much, and thank you to my team that is behind this presentation.

John Schellnhuber Now, I fully agree with demonstrations. Actually, what Francis Kéré showed us is really breathtaking, so beautiful. It takes from local resources. You have to see it so that you can believe it is possible. I have another question, which is about the broader bioeconomy. As you said, it is not just wood. We can do fantastic things with wood, but there are other biobased materials. Could you give us a few words on that?

Andreja Kutnar I would say that also other renewable materials, which I just emphasized, are often used in combination with some fossil-based materials. That's the way we are actually creating durable materials or some properties that are needed for certain application purposes. There is the opportunity for us to make a change, to create completely natural base materials. And of course, there is the question of the amounts that are available. In Europe, we have enough wood (Nabuurs et al. 2018). We often today also of course use it with fossil-based materials such as adhesives and coatings. This should be changed in the future. We should turn wood-based materials into a completely natural base. With other natural renewable materials, we have the task of finding their use in the built environment, despite their lower availability in terms of amounts, leading to better performance of a building, from the energy efficiency to the well-being of the built environment as such.

1 Koper's Servite Monastery, Santorijeva 9, Koper/Capodistria. A cultural monument of national importance according to the Decree (Official Gazette of the Republic of Slovenia no. 81/99, 55/02, and 16/08 – ZVKD-1) (Koper—Monastery Santorijeva 9 [ESD 8346]). The building was built in 1492 and was declared a cultural monument of national importance in 1999.

References

Burnard, Michael D., and Andreja Kutnar. 2015. "Wood and Human Stress in the Built Indoor Environment: A Review." *Wood Science and Technology* 49, no. 5: 969–86. https://doi.org/10.1007/s00226-015-0747-3.

Nabuurs, Gert-Jan, Eric J. M. M. Arets, and Mart-Jan Schelhaas. 2018. "Understanding the Implications of the EU-LULUCF Regulation for the Wood Supply from EU Forests to the EU." *Carbon Balance and Management* 13, no. 18. https://doi.org/10.1186/s13021-018-0107-3.

Panjek, Aleksander. 2015. *Kulturna krajina in okolje Krasa: o rabi naravnih virov v novem veku.* Koper, Slovenia: Založba Univerze na Primorskem. www.hippocampus.si/ISBN/978-961-6963-35-0.pdf.

USGBC. 2011. *Green Building and LEED Core Concepts Guide*. Washington, DC: United States Green Building Council.

5

rural is global

Xu Tiantian

Thank you. I am Xu Tiantian, I am an architect from Beijing, China [DnA_Design and Architecture]. Thank you very much for this opportunity. It is really my great honor to speak at PAS and present my work.

Asia is the most populated continent in the world. In the past two decades, Asia has gone through a rapid urbanization and economic growth process. At the same time, the Asian continent also faces rising environmental and social challenges caused by the increasing gap between urban and rural regions. As architectural practitioners, we have mostly been working in rural regions. In this process, architecture integrates with local context and heritage as a systematic and sustainable strategy—a healing treatment to restore the cultural heritage of Indigenous people, reduce the environmental impact, and rebuild urban and rural economic circulation. [My] presentation includes our three regional practice cases in the southern region of China. Each one concentrates on local issues and resources, to engage local communities and to provide sustainable solutions.

Fig. 5.1 Wang Jing Memorial Hall aerial

So the first chapter is in Songyang County, a typical agricultural county in China, which was losing its rural population and facing economic decline. We proposed architectural acupuncture as a systematic and sustainable rural strategy to help the region regain its rural self-confidence with a minimal intervention approach. A public program was introduced to each village according to its cultural context and heritage, applied with vernacular material and building techniques. Acupuncture integrates the village with nature, restores rural identity, and stimulates local economic development. For example, culture and history can restore the legacy of the ancient Wang Village, which has been totally surrounded by modern factories since the 1990s.

Fig. 5.2 Wang Jing Memorial Hall interior

A new memorial hall in the heart of the village is dedicated to the ancestor Wang Jing, an imperial scholar from the Ming Dynasty, to restore pride and honor. The articulation of the building not only creates a temple-like interior to walk through the life story of the

Fig. 5.3 Hakka Indenture Museum

Fig. 5.4 Shimen bridge and river

ancestor, but also frees up the central space to accommodate multiple functions. The new Memorial Hall has revealed pride and honor within the village, which also brought back the motivation and inspiration for villagers to further initiate new cultural programs and set up small businesses.

In a mountain village, a new rural museum is [used] to restore Hakka Indenture history. The Hakka Indenture collection in this Hakka village is a valuable cultural archive as the largest Hakka Indenture collection in the country. This museum also provides an opportunity to revive a lost craftsmanship: the traditional masonry building technique. The building has become a monument, reflecting the history of Hakka Indenture with the local masonry technique. The museum is also a summer pavilion open to both villagers and visitors. All these projects require light maintenance with low-tech natural lighting and ventilation, as sustainable public buildings. The new museum has inspired new investment to convert the adjacent vacant houses into homestay businesses and crafts workshops, which also provides new employment opportunities for villagers, especially women in this village.

Fig. 5.5 Shimen bridge

The abandoned infrastructure is also a valuable local resource that could be reused to restore the local identity. With the new bridge for vehicles built nearby, the old Shimen bridge was eventually abandoned and was about to be demolished. So we proposed to renovate the existing structure and add a new timber canopy. The unsafe infrastructure has been converted into a pedestrian bridge, reconnecting it to villages across the river, like the traditional launch bridge functioning as the meeting point for the local community. The new Shimen bridge also becomes a shared, multifunctional public space. It also provides a viewing platform for the adjacent 1,000-year-old ancient water dam. In ancient times, the two villages across the river used to be one village and were eventually separated into two by floods. This new Shimen bridge becomes the symbol to reunite two villages once again.

Fig. 5.6 Sugar factory (previous page)

In the rural region, the villages share a similar agricultural lifestyle, but almost every village has its own unique product, which is both intangible cultural heritage and an economic resource. In the case of Xing Village, brown sugar local products became the economic backbone of the area. Unlike other traditional villages, Xing maintained a rather steady population and agricultural production that generated sufficient income for the village to build new modern houses. The brown sugar production became the key element of the village's heritage.

The traditional cooking process is a striking performance, but family workshops were in poor condition. This new factory was programmed to engage family workshops as a collective economic entity to operate the factory. The improved production conditions also ensure an upgraded product quality to fit with healthy food requirements. The main production space is conceived as a central stage to showcase the traditional brown sugar production as a live performance, which also restored pride within the community for this unique agricultural tradition. The new factory, tailored for production and public education, has elevated the price of sugar and the village's income.

Over 50 villagers resettled back in their hometown. Many joined the sugar production union. The improved income has inspired more

Fig. 5.7 Tofu factory exterior

villagers to engage with the local ecological sugarcane plantation. The factory also functions as a village cultural center during the non-production season. In rural practice, [architecture] often requires multifunctional, more adaptive, resilient, and efficient interventions to achieve cultural, social, and economic sustainability.

Caizhai Village has always been known for the best tofu production in the county. [We designed] a new factory at the entrance of the village as a collective economic entity to engage individual family workshops as shareholders. All the production spaces are designed and equipped to upgrade traditional tofu products, fitting with food certificate standards. As the factory supplies tofu as a healthy food to local communities, it has also become a field trip educational workshop. The factory is an alternative rural museum with production as a live exhibition and performance. The covered walkway, inviting visitors to observe traditional tofu making, is an open leisure space for both visitors and villagers.

Fig. 5.8 / Fig. 5.9 Tofu factory interior

Fig. 5.10 Quarry 9 in the evening

The building requires simple maintenance. It is energy-saving, because it adopts natural lighting, natural ventilation and a rainwater collection system, promising a moderate economic lifestyle while maintaining regional cultural characteristics. The tofu factory not only is sustainable in its construction and maintenance, but also promises far-reaching societal resilience. The new production condition and increased circulation have improved both the quality and the price of the village's tofu product. After its completion, around 30 young villagers returned home from cities to join the production union. The factory has also inspired more ecological agriculture to ensure the quality of raw material for production.

Dwellings in rural regions are often the opposite of urban ones. Shangtian Village, whose history can be traced back 600 years, was becoming a depopulated village, with only a few elders remaining. Many houses are vacant and many have been abandoned for years due to the population drop. The village transformation was the first to reach common agreement with the local community, and then to renovate and convert the vacant houses as a shared homestay business owned by the village community. This also provides a new alternative living for urban residents.

The architectural design respects the history and preserves the village's original fabric by using traditional building techniques and craftsmanship. At the same time, a new hybrid collective rural economic entity is formed to protect the ownership and the village's potential economic value, which also avoids inequity created by urban investments. Villagers become shareholders with the assets of their properties. Those remaining in the village can also participate as employees. This also introduces a more diversified rural economy and attracts local talent and young villagers back home. With this new reform of the hybrid village collective economic entity, the Shangtian Village Transformation has established a new social structure that supports individual villagers who are often left behind in a market economy.

Our second chapter is located in Jingyun County with the adaptive reuse of abandoned quarries. The project provides a model example for the overall 3,000 abandoned quarries in the region to restore the interrupted nature and ecology, and to reuse the quarries as alternative public spaces with new possibilities. The design stimulates sustainable, future-oriented development that brings improvements to the stressed ecosystem. The reuse of these abandoned quarries also reconnects the local community with its 1,000 years of quarrying history and heritage in a sentimental dimension.

Fig. 5.11 Quarry 9 theater

The planning works with a cluster of adjacent quarries to provide supporting facilities for the scenic district. As such, the project also reduced the number of new buildings and the environmental impact of new constructions. It combines aspects of landscape planning, interior design, artistic installations, and social planning with economic revitalization of the rural area. The construction phase of each quarry lasts six months, including geotechnical reinforcement and architectural intervention. Both the construction time and the cost are less than for a new public building. So far, we have completed three quarries.

The first quarry of the cluster was the request and desire of local quarry workers and the community, who wished to provide a stage to demonstrate quarrying as a local manufacturing technique and historical heritage. Our design is a minimal intervention, with only necessary traces to reveal the quarry as a new rural public space of collective memory.

The second quarry is designed as a new quarry theater because of its acoustical quality and spatial reverberation effect. The conceptual position and the use of local resources determined the approach. The sensitive strategy adapted to local needs transforms the negative legacy of exploitation of natural resources into a symbol of hope in the rural hinterland.

The third quarry is a combination of a modern public library and a Chinese study dedicated to the local calligraphy context and spirit of literati. By adapting the concept of the “Book Mountain” from an ancient Chinese saying, the notion of design connects to a sense of retro and cultural metaphors from different dimensions of time and

space, at the same time reusing the quarry as a contemporary public platform.

The ruins caused by exploitation develop into a stage for culture that brings a new perspective to village communities in the region, both ecologically and economically. The Fujian *tulou* is a typical traditional building typology in Fujian province, in the southeast region of China, built between the 15th and 20th centuries. It is a technically sophisticated and self-sustainable defensive building for communal living in a highly sensitive setting in mountain valleys.

In 2008, 46 Fujian *tulou* were listed as World Cultural Heritage by UNESCO. There are still 1,000 *tulou* buildings in the region left unattended, vacant, or abandoned. This is our current chapter and challenge: to revitalize these ancient traditional buildings to improve and upgrade the living conditions for the original inhabitants, the Indigenous Hakka or Minnan people, and to convert the abandoned *tulou* buildings into modern public facilities with adaptive reuse.

Compared with the often large-scale developments or iconic landmark buildings in the urbanization process, the strategy targeting

Fig. 5.12 Book Mountain, readers

Fig. 5.13 Tulou buildings exterior

Fig. 5.14 Tulou building interior (next page)

rural issues is a rather micro-scale and human-centered approach. The issue of the rural is global, but a systematic local-scale intervention could become the strategic and sustainable solution. It also challenges architects to expand perspective, to identify issues, and to initiate collaborations.

Thank you.

三姐妹客栈

乡约土楼餐馆
乡约客栈
土楼特产专卖

6

indigenous planning in amazonia

Ana María Durán Calisto

It is a true honor to be here with you. From the perspective of Latin America, the way we feel right now is that since the process of modernity began in the 16th century (Wallerstein 2011), we have been turned into a hinterland of faraway cities and places extremely predatory of our resources. Latin Americans talk of suffering from ecocide, genocide, and epistemicide, in particular, Indigenous movements. Today I focus on epistemicide, by bringing forward the ontological wave (known as "the ontological turn") now happening within the field of anthropology, and I try to bring it into the field of architecture and city-making.

Whether we like it or not, our discipline [architecture], as much as it is liberating and as much as education can be a liberating force, can also be a blinding force. We have disciplinary blinders. I realized that when I had to face Amazonia and did not know how to approach it; I did not have the conceptual, technological, epistemological, or ontological tools to address the tropical rain forest from the perspective of urbanization and architecture. I had to go into other fields to try to understand it. So I turned to anthropology, however colonialist that field has been and can still be. However, it has been a conduit for me to understand Amazonia. But more than anything, just engaging with communities in the region has been paramount.

In order for my presentation not to be extractive academia, I would like to acknowledge, first of all, that all that I am going to present does not come from me. It comes from the Amazonian people; they and their history are the true and primary source. It also comes from modern archaeologists, who have been undertaking a century-old journey into the deep past of Amazonia.

I greatly appreciate [the work of archaeologists] because you have to be a bit insane to be a modern archaeologist in Amazonia. The region is shrouded in myth. It has been constructed as a pristine environment, as a "terra nullius": appropriated as an ahistorical space, frozen, with nomadic tribes running around in the rosy Stone Age. This could not be further away from the true history of Amazonia, which I would like to talk about because it is in that deep history of the Americas that I have found hope for the future. And sorry to disappoint, but I have not found that in technology. I have not found it in technocratic approaches, which only exacerbate mining in Latin America, and exacerbate the type of international development that I do not believe in anymore—international development that is the very cause of the ecocide, the genocide, and the epistemicide we are discussing.

In terms of Amazonian ontologies that I would share with you today, let us start with the image of the city. The city we have in our brain is full of preconceptions, the assumptions that came to us through our learning, our knowledge, and our eyes—that matrix that allows us to perceive the world or not to perceive the world. This is the image: We are in Rome. The city is a cell surrounded by a wall. All urbanists talk about this famous wall. It can grow, it can become multiple walls. The city is compact. It traditionally has some agricultural production areas within its walls. For military purposes, in case of a siege, people must feed themselves. Rome had some orchards within its walls, but for the most part there is a binary division embedded in this vision of the city: between the urban and the rural, or between the urban and the hinterland beyond (the mountain or the forest). This is not the case in Amazonia.

In the Americas, this predatory relationship between the urban and the rural, and the hinterlands (these modernities), began with the Spanish Empire and my ancestors' conquest and colonization of the Americas. I have both Spanish and Indigenous blood running in me. The city of Potosí[1] is an important symbol for Latin America to this day, because it is precisely about this extractivism for the benefit of a metropolis an ocean away. The way our whole region was structured geopolitically is expressed in Potosí: a territory urbanized to export raw materials across the Atlantic. This was the first global market. In the 16th century, the Spanish Empire established this transoceanic global system, with the Philippines on one side bringing in products from China and other Asian nations; Mexico as the navel of the world; and Europe on the receiving side. However, this is a system, a model, established in the 16th century that has only been exacerbated by what we call global capitalism. The difference now is that there is no investment in the land and its peoples, just extraction.

Fig. 6.1 The oil-boom town of Lago Agrio (Nueva Loja), Ecuador

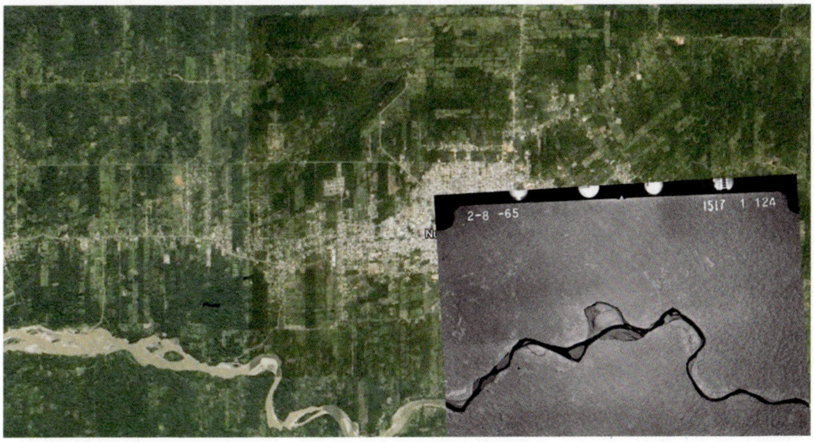

The neoliberal version of this geopolitical system is designed exclusively to extract and not to invest anything—or only a minimum—in the region. [The Global North] lends [the Global South] money through development banks like the World Bank, the International Monetary Fund, and the Inter-American Development Bank. These work [to fuel and finance the development of] the infrastructures for extraction. Billions of dollars go into highways that primarily benefit oil and mining companies, large ranching enterprises, and plantations. The same goes for hydroelectric infrastructures. Not much goes into investing in what is needed, like public education and public health. Investment goes into building infrastructure for further extraction, which benefits private and "state-owned" corporations. We extract, most of the revenues flow out of our region, and we are left with all the "negative externalities," as economists call them. I love this expression. We are left with only the negative externalities ... [ecocide, genocide, and epistemicide].

That is what we face as a region. I grew up in this world of globalization and have experienced firsthand the ecocide of my country, of its Amazonian hinterlands. Figure 6.1 is an aerial photograph from 1965, when Texaco was looking for oil—not just Texaco, but a consortium with Gulf. Several oil companies were looking for oil in Ecuadorean Amazonia, Colombian Amazonia, Peruvian Amazonia, and Bolivian Amazonia. Many still are. The black-and-white picture shows how the jungle used to be, and below, you can see how it is now. Urbanization in Amazonia is 80 percent informal, and it has exploded (Davis 2006; UN-Habitat 2003). It is basically a system of

Fig. 6.2 / Fig. 6.3 Sucumbíos Province, Ecuador, satellite image and official map demonstrating entropic occupation

informal urban striations, of forest favelas. The Amazonian forest has been favelized since the era of developmentalism, with its highways, massive deforestation, and "colonization" plans. It is important to understand that this entropic occupation was, to a large extent, planned. Colonization schemes designed to accommodate the landless of the region as Amazonia was used as an escape valve to avoid land reform in areas where the concentration of land was in the hands of members of the government or their friends.

This is simply one more manifestation of a global phenomenon: the favelization of the so-called Global South. You can see the evolution and the history. [Figure 6.1] is Lago Agrio, where the first oil rig was placed by Texaco in Ecuador. This is one dot in a system of oil extraction that has spread throughout Ecuadorean Amazonia, and is also spreading into the whole of the Andean or Upper Amazonia, which is one of the most biodiverse regions in the world. If you could look at a map of the oil blocks that are enclosing Amazonia today, you would be terrified. While we are sitting here talking about the future, forests, wood, biomaterials, and climate change, oil companies are still planning, with our vassal nation-states, the geometries of extraction. Politicians who don't abide by the rules get, one way or another, ousted or are prevented from ruling. Our vassal states are already planning to extract oil and metals in the whole of Andean Amazonia, which is already subdivided into oil and mining concession blocks.

I did not come here to tell you a story of doom and gloom that you all already know, because I believe in hope. We know this story well. Let us move to a story of hope, that is, to the role of women of all ages everywhere, but particularly Indigenous women, in the plight to protect territories from extractivism. Women play a very important role in the Indigenous movement, and the story of hope definitely intensifies in the Indigenous world of resistance. Some Indigenous groups choose to collaborate with extractivism, and have good reasons to do so in the face of inevitability, or the hope it will bring them greater well-being, or in some cases because they succumb to bribes or coercive tactics. That is why so many of us are looking at this world right now. When you overlap the map of the Amazonian forest with the map of the Indigenous communities and territories, you will see a high correlation between the presence of Indigenous people and healthy forests. Not that Indigenous populations have not partaken in deforestation; they have, and very often it is to be able to claim the land as rightfully theirs.

However, in Figure 6.2 and Figure 6.3, you can see how the privatized areas, the enclosed areas, highly correlate with deforestation, and the areas that you see there in green are all communes, in particular Quechuan chacras and managed forests.[2] You see, Amazonians are designers and builders of forests. While we talk about the difference between indoors and outdoors as a binary condition, Native Americans have been architects of the outdoors above everything else. In fact, it is fascinating to read the texts of the 17th-century Jesuits, who were oftentimes the first Europeans to penetrate the region. Many describe the phobia of Native Americans for enclosed spaces. In the Andes, capillas posas designed as semi-enclosed spaces served the purpose of bringing new converts into the temples while avoiding their aversion to fully enclosed containers (Gutiérrez 2002). It is here that we see one of many sociospatial (and temporal) manifestations of two ontologies clashing.

Fig. 6.4 Chacras on the Napo River of Ecuadorean Amazonia

Over time, one ontology has completely and systematically erased the other: *You are savage, you are primitive, and you do not have knowledge. I will develop you, I will civilize you, I will evangelize you, I will teach you.* This is the beginning of global hegemony, of the monocultures of the land and the monocultures of the mind, as Vandana Shiva would summarize it. This systematic erasure, from my perspective, is the erasure of the last hope we have to think of the future differently, polyculturally, regeneratively, which is the thinking that Amazonians have been enacting for thousands of years in their historical ecologies of abundance.

These networks of chacras you still see in the forest are the patrimony we should be caring for and protecting. It is not forests that need conserving, but the support of the people who build them. Amazonia is highly anthropogenic, and that has been proven by all sorts of scientists. Now these networks of chacras and the people who have the knowledge to design them are being overrun by the oil blocks, and I worry that they will be completely disrupted, if not exterminated, as they have been systematically for centuries.

The field of archaeology, particularly the highly multidisciplinary approach of historical ecology, is contributing extremely important knowledge, as it clearly demonstrates that the original nations of the Americas, and Amazonians in particular, have been enhancing the territories in which they live for millennia. Their systems were so complex that the Western mind is only now beginning to fully grasp them. Here we can see some images of Bolivian Amazonia, of its famous Llanos de Moxos. There were countless forest islands in this

region, and lakes. We originally thought they were completely natural, as is the case with most cultural territories of the original nations. The areas in green-gray are forest islands. They are all artificial. This is monumental from the ecosystem perspective, as monumental as anthropogenic and highly productive Amazonian cultural forests. This is a brilliant water management and agroecological system. You can see that it is interconnected by causeways, roads, and raised fields; these linear land formations are *chinampas*, also known as *camellones* or *waru waru* (raised agricultural fields in English). There are many ways of naming this agricultural management system in flooding areas, and it could be a brilliant method, in terms of the relationship between water and soil, for managing the transformation we face with climate change. Amazonians were wonderfully innovative when it came to inhabiting these areas through floating cities, raised fields, and other nature-based technologies. Cities in Amazonia also incorporated aquaculture and agriculture—forest agriculture. Do you see how the image of the city fixed in our brains comes from Mesopotamia and the Mediterranean, and not from Amazonia and its eco-logic? Even our idea of agriculture comes from a specific input territory: patches of products planned in geometric landscapes. However, agriculture in Amazonia is very different. The forest is agricultural. The forest is cultivated, has multiple useful species, is always polycultural, and is incredibly rich, so rather than depleting biodiversity, it enhances it.

Amazonian agriculture is also based on the creation of soils, known as *terra preta do índio* (Indian black earth) in Portuguese. Soils are enhanced and engineered on the one hand by biocharring, or smoking

Fig. 6.5 System of residential and/or ceremonial nodes in the urban agroecologies of the Llanos de Moxos, Bolivia

biomass, and on the other through the accumulation of discarded biomaterials (middens). Everything in Amazonia goes back into nature. What we are finding out now, thanks to Lidar,[3] a laser-based and aerial surveying technology capable of penetrating clouds and forests, is that Amazonia was highly populated and highly urbanized, with a very different type of urbanization. You can see [in Figure 6.5] an Arawak agroecological constellation. I believe this is the way to move forward in the tropics—in the Congo Basin, in Southeast Asia, in Amazonia—and maybe also the way to move forward in temperate areas: we should reverse the equation. Rather than the North telling the South what to do, maybe the South should suggest what the North could do. With Lidar, we are finding cities in Amazonia that are 10 times larger than the largest ones in the Andes. What is incredible about these cities is that they are dense yet dispersed, interconnected constellations. They are designed from a communal yet regional perspective, based on the interweaving of autonomous and complementary socio-ecologies that continuously exchange products, knowledge, and culture, which intermarry but can also go to war. It is important to understand that this is conceived as a society of nature, so to speak: animals and plants are active members of a community that is conceived beyond the human and where all manifestations of being, be they tangible or intangible, have a voice and a right to exist.

Let me show you a larger image of the agro-urban constellation of the Llanos de Moxos. When I read an article published last month by Heiko Prümers et al. (2022), archaeologists who have been studying the region for a long time, I couldn't help feeling extremely excited. They have proven that these were cities in their own right, in the tropical sense. Another solid example is provided by the Kuikuro villages and culture. Michael Heckenberger, an American archaeologist, has been studying the ethnohistory of the Kuikuro in the Upper Xingu of Brazil. He explains that we need to interpret current Kuikuro villages as shrunken, postcolonial versions of past, huge agroecological constellations, in a fractal, multi-scalar fashion of self-iteration through cyclical time. It is important to understand that the large and widespread populations of Amazonia that occupied the basin in the 16th and even 17th centuries, described by the first European explorers of the region and by the Jesuits and other missionaries, became disconnected, fugitive systems of what we term today "Indigenous groups in voluntary isolation." Amazonians understood early on that contact with the newcomers brought them pestilent "black clouds of smoke" that decimated their groups. The vast networks of interconnected chiefdoms or clans became purposely isolated, fugitive communities, interconnected through trails or water routes invisible to the Western eye, living in hiding from slave raids and epidemics. Isolation, in Amazonia, is a colonial phenomenon. The Arawak diaspora is a testament to the scale of the expansion of Amazonians and the extensive presence of their populations in the region until the 16th and 17th centuries. Large-scale, even intercontinental, interconnection is a precolonial phenomenon that persists in a shrunken and "clandestine" form (under the radar). Arawak cities, for example, were highly interconnected agroecological constellations with several tiers of hierarchy. Nevertheless, resources and power (in the sense of governance) were much better distributed.

Dark earths are an important index of settlement in Amazonia, and they are being mapped at a continental scale as well. They are present in fluvial and interfluvial areas. They constitute a "nature-based" technique like any other characteristic of the Americas, such as the chinampas (raised fields), forest islands, mound systems, *cochas*

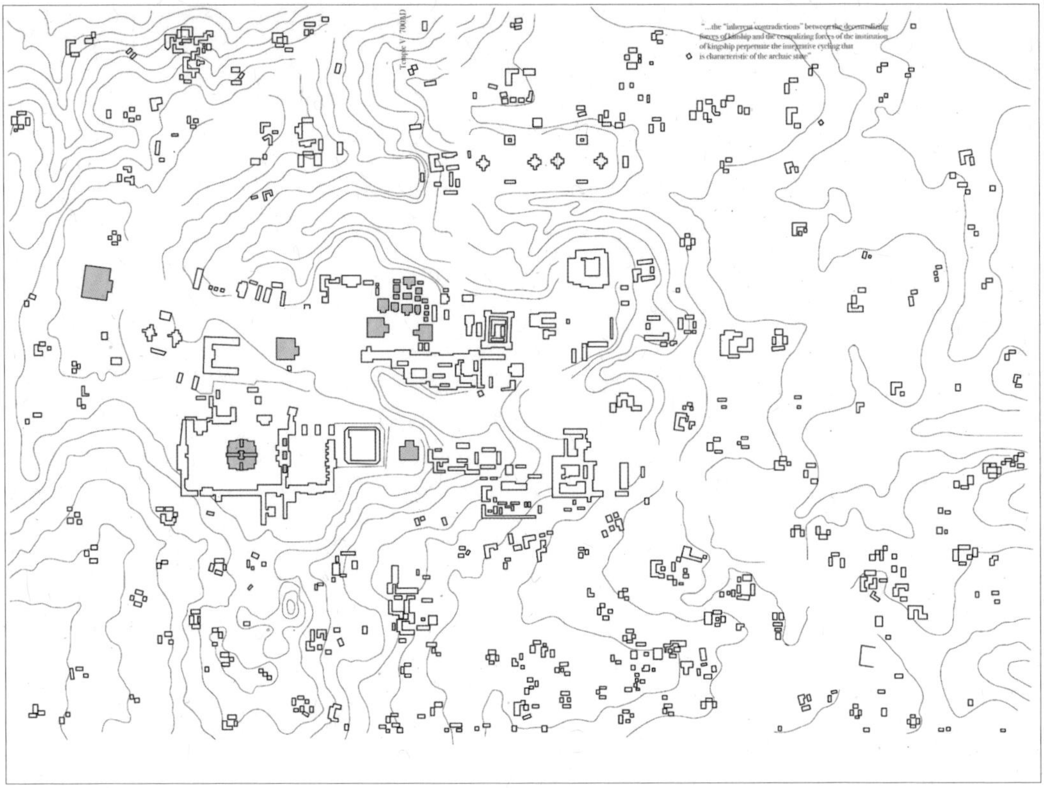

(anthropic lagoons or swamps), or terraced fields, among others. In Acre, since Brazilian archaeologist Alceu Ranzi first described them, hundreds of geoglyphs are being mapped. A very different vision of the Amazonian past is being registered by historical ecologists.

Analogous patterns can be perceived in the Mayan world. In Caracol, for example, known for its ceremonial center, archaeologists Diane and Arlen Chase conducted a Lidar study of its "suburban" areas. Alas! What emerged was the constellation of a regional city interconnected to other centers within a territorial constellation, in fractal fashion analogous to the one being unveiled for Amazonia. In the Lidar images, you can see all the subcenters and the residential ecological units that make up these fascinating cities. In Mesoamerica, as in Amazonia and the Andes, you find a variation of the same underlying pattern. The form varies as it adapts to a different ecology and expresses a different culture, yet the drive is the same: the collective creation of an abundant, agro- and biodiverse habitat.

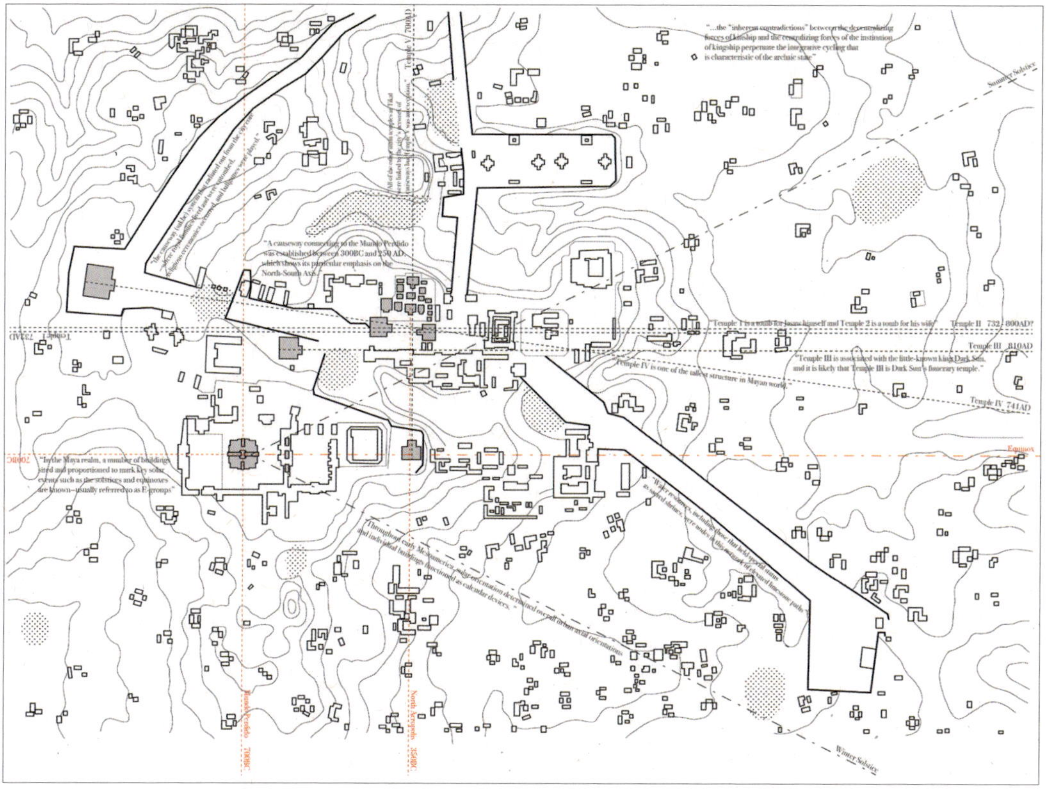

Fig. 6.6 / Fig. 6.7 Tikal, Guatemala. Note the constellations of dispersed, interconnected communities that support a regional system of productive habitat design and construction.

What I find fascinating is that in these agro-urban systems, you encounter a "type" of city that is simultaneously open and closed, rural and urban, local and regional, natural and artificial. There is no linear narrative that can explain these cities. They are completely multifunctional. The linear narrative of the West (from wild to rural to urban, from primitive to civilized) is useless in explaining these cities. They are hierarchical, but at the same time, they are horizontal. All the binaries that dominate the way we currently think about cities break down in these diffuse, low-density urbanisms. I call them agroecological and regional urban constellations, for lack of a better term, because when I use *city*, I often hear the response: No, Ana María, these are not cities, there were no cities in Amazonia. They are indeed not cities within the European ontology of the city. They are indeed cities, the cities of another ontology of the urban that is profoundly ecological in its design and making.

It is in these types of agro-urban constellations that we may find answers for the future, for a new cycle of the past and the present.

Of course, these nodes could not be interconnected by cars propelled by fossil fuels. We don't need to build highways. We don't need to copy the fossil fuel model, which has been so profoundly devastating to Amazonia. As Francis Kéré said: The Global South loves the Global North. It wants to look like it and wants to develop in its image, but that's exactly what we should not do. I hope the Global North understands that it must stop reproducing—through bilateral and multilateral organizations, development banks, and cooperation agencies—a technocratic model of development that dooms Latin America, Africa, and Southeast Asia to subserviently provide raw materials for the benefit of the North, at the expense of a genocide and ecocide. Ultimately, the extermination that feeds the global economy is imperiling the life of all.

With that, thank you so much.

John Schellnhuber Thank you, Ana María Durán Calisto, for opening our eyes to an alternative way of creating wealth, social cohesion, and so on. I wonder, first of all, whether we should look at this as an alternative narrative of circular economy, of being in equilibrium among ourselves and with nature. I wonder whether you have ever wondered, What if? What if the conquistadores had not arrived in the late 15th/16th century? What if fossil fuels had not underpinned global capitalism? How do you imagine this diversity of cultures would have developed? Would they have also gone on to a superlinear, nonlinear, exponential growth or something like that, or would they have just stayed in some equilibrium?

Ana María Durán Calisto I would guess the communities would have kept their system, because they have preserved it. The resistance has been huge. It is a living system, undergoing a new cycle. The First Nations would not have resisted all these centuries of exploitation had they not a system of organization that is founded on the interconnection of their communal system. It is shocking to me to find, for example, in the fringes of megacities like São Paulo, the Mbyá Guaraní oasis, surviving whole in the midst of immense pressure. They refuse to follow our model because they consider it absurd and doomed. How have they managed to live in a forest with São Paulo looming upon them? That says everything, I feel. In fact, thanks to their philosophy, we now have inscribed in the Ecuadorean constitution, since 2008, the rights of nature. This is an Indigenous concept; mestizos have simply given it a legal form within the constitution. We speak about circular economy, permaculture—these are all Indigenous concepts. Europe was Indigenous too.

We have 5,500 years or more of urban history in the Americas, and I think that the rights of nature come from its deep ontology and are related to another notion, that of *sumak kawsay* in Kichwa,[4] which in English would be "the good life" or "the plentiful life," in Spanish *el buen vivir*—an ancient concept that has, unfortunately, been politicized and is associated with the Latin American left. When I look at these ancient cities, I think, Oh my! This is the *sumak kawsay*. Another thing that I find amazing about these cities is that they enhance biodiversity, cultural diversity, and linguistic diversity. There are currently more than 330 languages spoken in Amazonia. Imagine how many thousands of languages existed in the Americas when the Europeans arrived. It feels like all this biodiversity, cultural diversity, and linguistic diversity is being sacrificed to one hegemonic way of doing and thinking, and now we do not know what to do, we do not have alternatives, and that is because we have been systematically dismantling them.

1 A city in Bolivia, regarded, in the 16th century, as the world's largest industrial complex, as a result of extensive silver ore extraction.

2 Amazonian polycultural orchards, highly agro- and biodiverse, as they are composed through a deep understanding of ecology and synergies between species, many of them useful.

3 Acronym for "light detection and ranging" or "laser imaging, detection, and ranging" (also LIDAR, or LiDAR; sometimes LADAR).

4 Quechuan language spoken across Colombia, Ecuador, and Peru.

References

Davis, Mike. 2006. *Planet of Slums*. London and New York: Verso Books.

Del Hierro, S. 2017. *Plan estratégico territorial para la zona de influencia del corredor Manta-Manaos en Sucumbíos, PLAN ZIMM-S*. Quito and Los Angeles: Pontificia Universidad Católica del Ecuador and CityLab UCLA.

Gutiérrez, R. 2002. *Arquitectura y urbanismo en Iberoamérica*. Naples, Italy: Guida Editori.

Prümers, Heiko, Carla Jaimes Betancourt, José Iriarte, Mark Robinson, and Martin Schaich. 2022. "Lidar Reveals Pre-Hispanic Low-Density Urbanism in the Bolivian Amazon." *Nature* 606: 325–28. https://doi.org/10.1038/s41586-022-04780-4.

UN-Habitat (United Nations Human Settlements Programme). 2003. *The Challenge of Slums: Global Report on Human Settlements*. London and Sterling, VA: Earthscan Publications.

Wallerstein, Immanuel. 2011. *The Modern World-System I: Capitalist Agriculture and the Origins of the European World-Economy in the Sixteenth Century*. Berkeley: University of California Press.

7

wetland: a future vernacular

Wael Al Awar

Good afternoon, everyone, and thank you for inviting me to be here. It's an honor amongst such great minds to be speaking from a perspective of only a practicing architect and not much of an academic. I think my inspiration as an architect and my true desire is to build in a new, sustainable way that can give meaning to the practice and the work I do.

Currently, I have offices in Dubai and Tokyo, and the work we produce is at different scales and for different programs, including, for example, mosques, museums, multidisciplinary cultural centers, and performance centers, as well as incubator spaces and private houses. I am here today not to explain my architectural practice, but mainly to focus on my research behind Wetland. I first presented Wetland at the Venice Architecture Biennale in 2021. It was a response to the question raised by Hashim Sarkis on how we live together, and as a practicing architect, it was important for me to address the relationship between humans and planet Earth. I felt that we had disconnected from the planet, that our systems had failed us, and that we needed to find new ways to reconnect with it.

First, how do I view the Venice Architecture Biennale? For me, the Venice Architecture Biennale is similar to the Mos Eisley cantina from *Star Wars*. It is a platform on which creatures from all over the world with different cultural backgrounds and ideologies come together to engage in discourse. I wanted to have a conversation that could engage everyone and that really addressed the immediate crisis we are currently living in. The title of the research is Wetland. As I go through the explanation of the work, you will understand why. This research was presented as curatorial work for the National Pavilion of the United Arab Emirates, and I also wanted to question the stereotypical images that we have of countries like the UAE, where actually 5 percent of the local geography consists of wetlands, which are the salt flats.

As you know, and as we have been discussing today, we are moving toward a global population of 11 billion people (Kunzig 2014; Santamouris and Vasilakopoulou 2021). How are we able to build our future cities with this exploding population? A Bill and Melinda Gates

Fig. 7.1 Camels traveling across salt flats

Foundation report from 2019 states that we will have to build the equivalent of one New York City every month over the next 40 years to meet that growing population. How do we do this, knowing that we are in a climate emergency and knowing that the construction industry is largely responsible for that emergency?

The construction industry is responsible for approximately 40 percent of the global CO_2 emissions, and cement alone is responsible for 8 percent. Today, we consume 30 billion tons of cement (*Nature* 2021, 597). If we grow to 10 billion people, we will be consuming 60 billion tons of cement per annum. So the mathematics don't add up. As a practicing architect, how am I going to build my next project? I desperately need to find a solution. Also, it is important to note that to produce one ton of cement, we produce one ton of CO_2. Cement is an archaic, dumb material. If it was invented today, no one would approve the ratio of one to one in any product.

This is something that I did not know as an architect until I started looking into this research. Also, today our construction mindset is based on an extraction methodology, so we consume our resources in order to build, and the construction industry has a great responsibility in terms of energy. Eighty-four percent of global energy still comes from fossil fuels, and only 11 percent comes from renewable energy (Ritchie, Roser, and Rosado 2022). We are very, very far behind.

Finally, excess waste. What is the responsibility of the construction industry in terms of waste? To put it in very simple mathematics, the responsibility, as we have already said, is about 40 percent. The modernist architect, I believe, did not have that challenge. The issue of the climate emergency and the issue of CO_2 is a recent phenomenon that the 21st-century architect has to tackle. Then the question becomes, what is my responsibility as a 21st-century architect and how can I tackle the situation in my practice?

At the Venice Architecture Biennale, a lot of pavilions turned to vernacular architecture—even everyone speaking here about wood and using wood. The Philippines pavilion presented a pavilion in sustainable wood, as did the USA, the Nordic countries, and others. But for me, coming from an office in Dubai, the vernacular architecture was using corals. How can I go back to using corals? Corals could only work for a population of 200 people, but for the current population, which is 10 million in the UAE and growing to 20 million in the next 10 years, how would I find a way that doesn't exist?

Fig. 7.2 Coral wall, traditional building material

I had to start thinking in a new way and to find the problem within cement. Can I find a solution to that problem? Once I started to look into the problem of cement, I understood that the main issue is in the glue, the binder, and in converting limestone to lime, which emits this tremendous amount of CO_2. So if I could find an alternative glue or binder, then maybe that would offer a solution. I had to turn to geography and geology to find a binder or an alternative glue.

In this quest and in walking around the landscape, I came across the sebkhas of the UAE. *Sebkha* is an Arabic word found in the English dictionary, meaning salt flat. I was immediately captivated by the cementitious crust of these salt flats. As I said, 5 percent of the UAE's environment is made from these sebkhas, which fall under the category of wetlands. I was certain there would be a glue within that cementitious layer that was binding the minerals together, so the question became, what is this glue, and can it replace lime in the cement mix for OPC (ordinary Portland cement)?

Sebkhas are not a UAE phenomenon. Of course, salt flats are global. You also find sebkhas in Ethiopia, in Tunisia, in the Mojave Desert in California, for example. In Bolivia, they are extracted as lithium. The lithium is mainly extracted to be used in Tesla car batteries and mobile phones. Then I also came across vernacular architecture in certain countries in North Africa that use sebkhas for construction.

Siwa is a town in Egypt, near the border with Libya. It's 800 years old and is built from sebkhas that were extracted from the ground. Again, this is contextual architecture. This could work only within its climatic condition. Sebkhas are a soluble salt, so in an area of heavy rain, it would not work; it would immediately dissolve. Funnily enough, I learned that even the architecture in *Star Wars* was

Fig. 7.3 Al Ruwais salt flats, United Arab Emirates

actually built from sebkhas—it is vernacular architecture of the past and not a stage set.

I learned much about sebkhas, minerals, and the different glues within them. Sebkhas are carbon sinks. They absorb CO_2. One square meter of sebkha absorbs more CO_2 than one square meter of rain forest. These are specifically the sebkhas in the Gulf region, because they have within them a microbial mat, a living organism, that allows for the absorption of CO_2. I definitely cannot promote the extraction of sebkhas in order to create the new architecture. I would be going against what I am trying to do. But what I learned is that the minerals within sebkhas can also be found in other resources.

Here I'm going really fast. Through a very lengthy process, we discovered that these minerals are all found in the reject brine of desalination water. The MENA region is responsible for 48 percent of global desalination. The UAE alone dumps the equivalent of 4,800 Olympic-sized swimming pools per day of rejected brine back into the Arabian Sea, and this is causing an environmental disaster (Landais 2009; Salman and Abubaker 2020). The salinity in the sea is increasing, and salt plus water equals battery. Heat is increasing. The corals have all died in the sea, as have many marine species.

We brought reject brine solutions into the office and started to experiment with them to see how we can create architecture with such a heavy saline liquid. The first, most obvious thing we learned was that if we suspend fabrics that work in tension into the reject brine over two or three days, they crystallize, and when we remove them, they start to work in compression. You could immediately start to create very quick structures from just submerging these fabrics into the reject brine solution. The problem with that is, again, these are soluble structures, meaning that they absorb humidity. If it rains, they will collapse. They cannot really be used as a replacement for cement. I really wanted to find a concrete kind of solution, and not only a halfway attempt.

There are other model studies that we did, so then I thought, okay, I can't do this, maybe I should start talking to biochemistry labs at

Fig. 7.4 / Fig. 7.5 Crystallization experiments at waiwai office

universities and they could help me understand more clearly salt compositions, the minerals, and how they could work. The first collaboration was with the American University of Sharjah, and we started extracting all the different minerals from the brine, understanding each salt by itself, and producing materials and finishes from all these different salts. Again, these were soluble attempts until we discovered that magnesium oxide is a salt that can be extracted from rejected brine and can form an insoluble crystal.

We started a collaboration with AMBER Lab, which is the Advanced Material Research Laboratory at New York University Abu Dhabi. In that research, instead of using lime, we started creating cement blocks with magnesium oxide extracted from the reject brine of desalination water. Now, this cement is a new system. It has new properties and new ways of thinking. In the first attempt, we realized that the compression strength is very, very low; then we learned that this system needs to be carbonated in order to gain structural strength, meaning it needs to absorb CO_2. It can absorb 18 percent of its mass in CO_2 in order to become structurally strong.

Fig. 7.6 Crystallization experiments at waiwai office

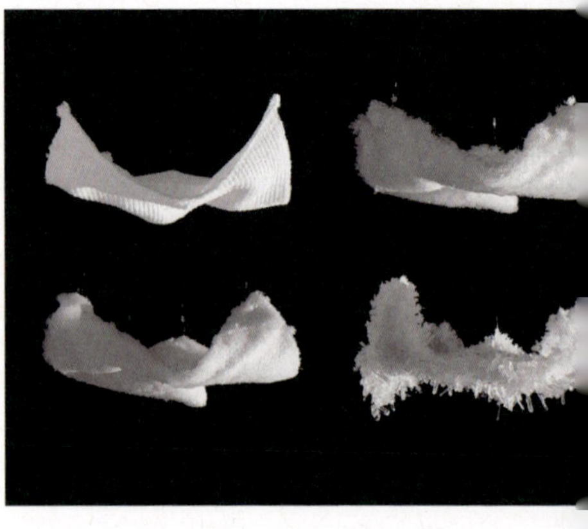

Here I will show you a video. You see the block that is non-carbonated and the block that is carbonated. Carbonation is not something fancy. All you have to do is expose the block to CO_2 for 72 hours. It could be from CO_2 tanks or it could be in a plastic bag at the exhaust of a car, and that would do the job. We wanted to present the material at the Architecture Biennale in Venice,

Fig. 7.7 Wetland prototype casting at the University of Tokyo (left)

Fig. 7.8 Wetland prototype at the University of Tokyo (right)

but we also wanted to ask ourselves the question, how will I present this in Venice? We need to question modern materials, we need to question our modern methods of producing space. I feel today that it is important that we bring back culture and identity into the production of architecture and space.

We began a collaboration with the University of Tokyo, two laboratories at that university, and we produced a prototype: a homage to the vernacular architecture of the UAE inspired by coral shapes. This would be the antithesis of modern architecture, since the modules are all drawn by hand into soil and then cast, so there is no drawing. There is no architect who is producing a set of drawings and dictating the final outcome of the process. Rather, students imagined what corals look like and drew this into soil and then cast them.

The first prototype was built at Tokyo University, but I was keen on vocational learning, so students from Tokyo University exchanged with students in the UAE and we built a second prototype in the UAE, before moving to the building of the prototype in Venice. At Venice, we presented under the title Wetland because sebkhas fall under the category of wetlands according to the Ramsar Convention of 1970. At the pavilion, we also exhibited photos taken by Farah Al Qasimi, an Emirati artist based in New York, that really captured the tension between landscape and industrialization. You can see in the background the desalination and energy plants. Through these photos, we wanted to bring forward the struggle between human and nature, and how we reconnect to the environment.

Fig. 7.9 Al Ruwais salt flats, landscape (next page)

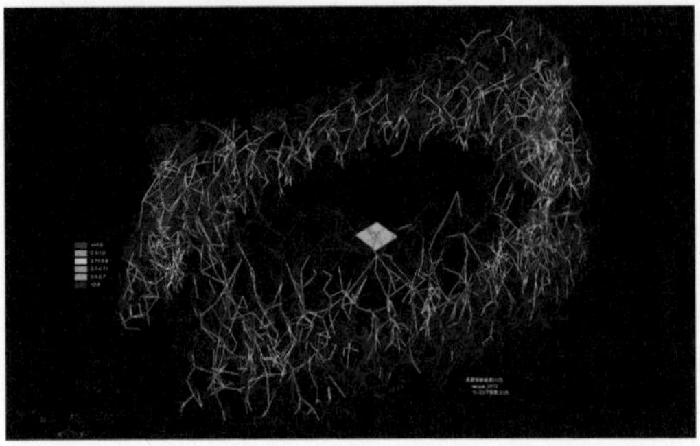

Fig. 7.10 Wetland prototype structural analysis at the University of Tokyo

Finally, we presented a prototype built from 2,400 modules, all produced in Venice. There was nothing shipped to Venice. We even took some of the sebkha sections in our suitcases. The dilemma was actually that, when we wanted to submit this to the Biennale, they wanted a structural verification drawing before we even produced the prototype, but the whole point is that we are redefining systems, and this system is about trying to build in new ways.

The Tokyo University Obuchi Lab actually programmed devices from the Wii. I will show you very quickly how it works. The builder wears a device on their wrist. This is where we merge high tech with low tech. This is where we take advantage of the technology we have today. Then we project a hologram of the outline of the form we want to build, because we had a limited number of units and had to ensure egress routes were correct.

You can see the builder in Figure 7.10. While they build, they wear a wrist device. When it lights up blue, it is within the model form. You can see a computer with a base station that is linked to Tokyo University. As we build, the sensors in the ceiling are continuously scanning the model and producing an as-built replica in the computer. We built this using seven layers. At every layer, we would have to stop for half an hour depending on the internet connection and get a verification that the structure was sound in order to start building the next layer, but even that was very simple. It was more about just adding one more block or just slightly twisting one block. Finally, we could have a structural verification model, but it came after the prototype was completed.

President Roberto Cicutto himself would come in during the construction and shake the modules to check how they would perform in public. As I said, finally we were able to build a prototype of 2,400 modules, all built through conversations and without a single drawing.

Thank you.

Sheela Patel I just wanted to tell you that in Mumbai, where I come from, our government for the first time has chosen desalination as a strategy to produce additional drinking water, versus extracting water from rural areas. I can ask them to get in touch with you to do something like this with the saline water.

Wael Al Awar I presented this research at UNESCO last year, where we brought in 52 delegate states, trying to bring countries from all over the world to help us with the continuation of the research. I think the whole world will move more and more toward desalination. We have a water crisis all over the world. Currently, Saudi Arabia is the largest desalinator, but surprisingly, the United States is the second largest (Johnston 2015). Chile is a very big desalinator too. I think countries that desalinate are countries that we could be cooperating with, but countries that have an abundance of trees should be looking at their own ways of building.

What I think we should be talking about is not, again, following the modern mindset of standardization and globali-

Fig. 7.11 Wetland exhibition, National Pavilion UAE, La Biennale di Venezia, 2021

zation, of one solution fits all. It does not work like that. It is about your community, your environment, your context, and what works for you. If you are mindful of your context, you are immediately mindful of other contexts.

Nathalie Jean-Baptiste Thank you very much for a great presentation. I am wondering if you can speak to the architects and the builders out there who do not have the luxury of doing the research that you've done, nor the funding, and who are under pressure to build, but want to build in a better way. What would be the first step? In continents such as Africa, we build fast. What would be the way to start?

Wael Al Awar That's a very good question. How would I say it? For this research, I got the funding by applying to an open call competition that was then adopted by the National Pavilion of the UAE. Then I got the funding to continue the research. I could not have funded it from my own pocket. I do believe, if someone has a great idea, there are a lot of open calls and opportunities out there. They can go to the right channels to get the necessary support. I know this is hard because, even after winning the Golden Lion, I still struggle to get funding, but nonetheless, I am sure there are mechanisms out there that will support.

Now, for young architects, they feel desperate, they feel worried, they ask, "How am I going to build?" I think you have to think small and incrementally, and not think that you're the only person who will have the only solution. It's about thinking long term. I know we do not have time, but if we don't think a little bit in the long term, then we will just stop in despair. It is about a certain mindset. Today, I showed you the projects we built. Are they carbon zero? No, they are not, but I know that, on the other hand, I am focusing on research that may, five years down the line, give me the methods and tools to build in better ways. You have to find that balance in operating.

References

Johnston, Chris. 2015. “Desalination: The Quest to Quench the World’s Thirst for Water.” *Guardian*, May 27, 2015. www.theguardian.com/technology/2015/may/27/desalination-quest-quench-worlds-thirst-water.

Kunzig, Robert. 2014. “A World with 11 Billion People? New Population Projections Shatter Earlier Estimates.” *National Geographic*, September 19, 2014. www.nationalgeographic.com/science/article/140918-population-global-united-nations-2100-boom-africa.

Landais, Emmanuelle. 2009. “Waste Dump Threatens Arabian Gulf.” *Gulf News*, June 14, 2009. https://gulfnews.com/uae/environment/waste-dump-threatens-arabian-gulf-1.72058.

Nature. 2021. Editorial, “Concrete Needs to Lose Its Colossal Carbon Footprint.” *Nature* 597 (September): 593–94. https://doi.org/10.1038/d41586-021-02612-5.

Ritchie, Hannah, Max Roser, and Pablo Rosado. 2022. “Energy.” *Our World in Data*. https://ourworldindata.org/energy.

Salman, Nour, and Rasha Abubaker. 2020. “MENA Water Desalination Market to Reach US$4.3 Billion by 2022.” WAM—Emirates News Agency, February 24, 2020. www.wam.ae/en/details/1395302826317.

Santamouris, Matthaios, and Konstantina Vasilakopoulou. 2021. “Present and Future Energy Consumption of Buildings: Challenges and Opportunities toward Decarbonisation.” *e-Prime: Advances in Electrical Engineering, Electronics and Energy* 1. www.sciencedirect.com/science/article/pii/S2772671121000024.

8

sustainable digitization and data democracy for urban transformation

Francesca Bria

I'm honored to be here. I would like to thank John Schellnhuber for giving me the privilege to speak in this inspiring conference and I am proud of President von der Leyen for being in Rome to open the first edition of the New European Bauhaus Festival.

In my contribution, I am going to talk about the need to democratize technology and to advance a value-driven technology and innovation agenda at the European level. I will also stress how it is important to combine the Green Deal with a Digital Deal, with a technology and data policy that can only start with people first, not technology first. I will give some examples that are mainly based on the work I have been doing in the past years as adviser to the United Nations on digital cities and digital rights, and as CTO of the city of Barcelona.

When we talk about advancing a technology agenda for Europe, we do not only mean accelerating the uptake of technological solutions, but instead starting from the required institutional, socioeconomic, and cultural changes needed. We are aware of the broader implications of today's digital industrial transformation, coupled with the multiple crises we are facing, in particular the climate and energy crises that impose a paradigm shift in our industrial and economic system.

We are experiencing one of the moments of greatest emergency and structural change in recent years. After more than two years of the pandemic, which has created both a social and an economic crisis, we are facing a serious energy crisis caused by the Russian invasion of Ukraine, which has sent energy prices skyrocketing. The effect is a new supply shock, and extreme volatility in food, metal, and commodity prices, with inflationary pressures due to more than two years of supply chain disruptions and raw material shortages—a macroeconomic framework that risks wearing down the purchasing power of households, the level of wages, and access to liquidity for businesses.

Behind this scenario, real systemic crises are emerging that have been dragging on for a few decades, in particular the crisis of unregulated globalization and the climate emergency. It is not by chance that the word of the year chosen by the Collins Dictionary is precisely *perma-crisis*. We are living in a condition of permanent emergency. To address the interconnected crises of pandemic, war, inflation, climate, and energy, we need massive investment in research, sustainable innovation, and low-carbon infrastructures by mobilizing and unleashing all available instruments in the entire EU bloc. This will most likely include easing state aid rules and pushing for a "Made in Europe" strategy with a "Sovereignty Fund" to mobilize massive fundings in key strategic projects for the climate transition in sectors such as batteries, photovoltaics, hydrogen, microprocessors, and critical materials.

These transformations also present an emerging geopolitical dimension, creating a real disruption of the global order, leading to a technological decoupling, a Great Silicon Divide springing up between East and West. This is accelerating a trade war between China and the United States that puts the already fragile global supply chains under pressure, starting from the shortage of microprocessors, a strategic component of any industrial chain and essential for a wide range of products, such as cars, household appliances, and electronics.

In this context, many countries, including Europe, are looking at strategic autonomy or technological sovereignty, requiring us to think in new ways about raw material extraction, technological and infrastructural dependencies, and postcolonial supply chains.

Transformative Innovation for the Green Deal

Against this background, radical and future-oriented political action seems even more urgent. Therefore, we should turn this crisis into an opportunity to redesign our society and the economy, to rethink our development model for the common good. The innovation we need should be seen as synonymous with a tangible change in existing economic models focused on biodiversity, sustainability, and strong scientific and technological skills.

However, we know that technology and digitization can also exacerbate existing problems. Artificial intelligence, massive computation,

Fig. 8.1 Visualization of superblock, Plaça Rocafort, Barcelona

robotization, and automation present new forms of power and will consume enormous environmental and human resources. The development of technologies such as 5G networks, cloud computing, and artificial intelligence infrastructures has become a national and global priority, since we realized that essential services of society, such as work, health care, and education, depend upon critical infrastructures owned and controlled by a handful of tech giants that are amassing a great amount of wealth and social power, presenting an industrial concentration unheard of in recent history.

Thus, it is not enough to accelerate digitization, we must also give it a direction that is to attain social and environmental sustainability. Access to connectivity—free, public, and accessible ultra-broadband—is to be considered a fundamental right of all citizens, and data and technology should be governed in a democratic way, preserving people's autonomy, human rights, and environmental standards.

To respond to the massive climate emergency, we need to decarbonize the economy and move toward a circular economy, developing a way of life and work that gives our planet a real chance to fight for the next generation. That's why Europe has created the European Green Deal, to have a legal basis to reach the climate goals of reducing net greenhouse gas emissions 55 percent by 2030 and reaching climate neutrality by 2050. To achieve these ambitious goals, we need huge investments in innovation and infrastructures. The International Energy Agency (IEA) estimates that more than

60 percent of the technologies necessary to achieve the goal of reducing CO_2 emissions by 2070 are already in the laboratory prototyping phase but with development stages still too low. A third of the €1.8 trillion investments from the NextGenerationEU Recovery Plan and the EU's seven-year budget will finance the European Green Deal, meaning green investments and reforms. The EU is also funding green projects from the regional aid scheme, as well as putting forward initiatives in areas such as renewable energy, green hydrogen, and next-generation batteries under the RePowerEU plan, which aims to transition Europe away from Russian fossil fuels and improve energy infrastructures. This massive investment capacity needs to be coupled with our ability to spend these resources well and channel them to the right projects and to the communities that need them the most.

So, we have the right legislation, normative frameworks, and investments to make the ecological transformation of our industrial system happen. But we know this kind of shift doesn't happen only with the right laws, investments, and financial taxonomies designed top-down. We need to bring people and communities along and we need to make it inclusive for people who live in different realities, such as working-class families and communities living in the Global South that are paying the highest price for the climate emergency. That's why the New European Bauhaus is a central part of Europe's future vision. It aims to unleash a grassroots movement and foster an interdisciplinary mindset to imagine and develop concrete projects on the ground that change people's lives and behaviors.

One hundred years ago, the Bauhaus was founded in Weimar, Germany, as a response to the cataclysm of the First World War, which led to a great upheaval in many different areas. New thinking comes from breaking down silos, just as the historical Bauhaus movement did. We will create a better tomorrow if art, science, and technology go hand in hand.

The New European Bauhaus will bring innovation to the market, with new products and services, new sustainable economic models, and new skills. New digital solutions have made our lives more convenient but have not yet transformed the physical environment where we live, work, and move. The climate crisis highlights the need for deeper decarbonization in all sectors and calls for transforming outdated business models into more sustainable ones. What we need now is a new wave of innovation, which should be synonymous with a tangible change of existing economic models centered around biodiversity, sustainability, and regenerative approaches based on the interconnection between living beings and their socio-ecological values.

A Data and Environment Deal That Starts from Cities

In order to fully engage people and communities, while addressing inequalities and the climate emergencies, we need to start from cities, with a vision of the smart city that does not start from technology but from the needs of people and the great urban challenges: sustainable mobility, the fight against climate change, affordable housing, education, and public health.

That's what I tried to do as CTO of Barcelona, to completely redefine what we call smartness today. It is about making sure that technology works for people and the environment. If cities consume 70 percent of global energy and 80 percent of food, and emit 75 percent of pollutants and greenhouse gases, while occupying only 3 percent of the planet's surface, how can we reduce their impact on the environment? The 2030 Agenda for Sustainable Development and the New Urban Agenda are two globally agreed agendas that can guide the achievement of sustainable urbanization, in line with the Paris goals.

Europe has the opportunity to become a global reference for decarbonization and democratic digitization, combining the European Green Deal and Europe's digital strategy and starting from cities, using the Recovery and Resilience Plans to make our cities greener and carbon neutral. Local administrations have the capacity, agility, and proximity to rapidly activate transformations; in many cases, they are already considered reference cities in sustainable mobility and in the green and digital transitions. Because of their closeness to citizens' real problems, cities are agents of social cohesion, seeking to overcome divides and inequalities with concrete policies.

Fig. 8.2 The Eixample, Barcelona (next page)

This is a wake-up call, an invitation to transform our cities toward climate neutrality, toward a circular economy vision, establishing a new relationship with nature, and designing a new way of working and balancing the time we spend at home and in the office. Which also means building sustainable homes with open spaces, urban gardens, and coworking spaces.

Cities such as Barcelona, Helsinki, Hamburg, Amsterdam, and Copenhagen have developed ambitious climate plans that put them at the forefront of the imperative of achieving climate neutrality by 2050 and reducing emissions by at least 55 percent by 2030.[1] Many cities are moving toward a circular economy vision, with large urban projects that follow the 15-minute city model that guarantees citizens proximity to essential services, such as in Paris, Barcelona, Milan, Helsinki, and Madrid, freeing up public land and the spaces of the historic center from cars and traffic, investing in a sustainable and shared mobility system, increasing the number of cycle paths and the capillarity of public transport.

Fig. 8.3 Women sitting on a bench in public space repossessed from motor vehicle traffic use

Barcelona, with the superblocks project, did something ambitious (2022), reclaiming a large percentage of public space and removing cars from the city center, thus reducing emissions and adapting to climate change. Now there are a series of neighborhoods (urban superblocks) that are self-sustaining, creating more opportunities to provide space for citizens and mitigating the lack of green areas. Many other cities are implementing re-naturalization projects by planting thousands of trees, investing in renewable energy, building efficiency, energy saving, and the creative reuse of waste.

To achieve this kind of green urban transformation, cities need to equip themselves with a digital infrastructure (connectivity, data, sensors, and platforms) that collects public data on electricity and heat consumption, mobility, water management, and pollution. This data is a new critical urban infrastructure, a common good (Bria 2018), that can be managed ethically and securely, preserving the privacy, rights, and digital sovereignty of citizens and at the same time guaranteeing access to start-ups, multi-utility providers, and companies to create value and new services in the public interest.

I focused my political action in Barcelona on this issue when I was the Councillor for Digitization and Innovation, creating a Data Office with 40 people and developing a decentralized data platform based on blockchain technology to give back control of data to citizens and encourage sharing to improve the city and create public value.[2] The Barcelona data strategy has become a model at a European and global level, as the United Nations has taken it as an example to be reproduced globally, via the Cities Coalition for Digital Rights.[3]

The effective move toward a net-zero economy entails planning and building with biobased materials, prioritizing policies such as energy and technological sovereignty, and integrating the collective intelligence of citizens in the decision-making process. Public representatives must learn to really listen to citizens and make them actively participate in political decisions, as we did in Barcelona, carrying out one of the largest participatory democracy experiments in the world, with hundreds of thousands of citizens participating in writing the government agenda and, thanks to participatory budget tools, also expressing their priorities with respect to the projects to be financed. This participation process was a success also thanks to a free software digital platform we developed (decidim.org), which today is used by over 100 cities and governments in 20 countries worldwide and by the European Union for the Conference on the Future of Europe.[4]

It is necessary to be able to actively involve the communities and the new generations. For example, the green transition is also about changing the way we live, consume, and work. Many young people care about the environment, protest for sustainability, but don't know how to implement these values in their daily lives; and they don't always know how to engage and change things in their neighborhoods and communities. This kind of transformation is a matter of democracy. We need the right regulation, standards, principles, and public digital infrastructures based on our common values.

If Europe has a chance to put forward a new model for digitization, it has to be value-based. In this digital transition, issues related to civil liberties, individual privacy, and the functioning of our democracy must be given central importance; we need a technology that is centered around human values and fundamental rights. This means preserving human rights in the digital age, embracing a model where technology and knowledge are accessed, governed, and used in a democratic way in order to mobilize collective action for the public interest.

If we need data to tackle all these challenges of society, we need to move away from a model where people's data is monopolized, owned, and monetized by a handful of companies, what Professor Shoshana Zuboff calls "the Age of surveillance capitalism" (Zuboff 2019). This is a paradigm where our data, which we produce every day, is continuously analyzed, manipulated, and traded in opaque digital marketplaces using algorithmic black boxes. If we want to preserve autonomy and information self-determination, we must

Fig. 8.4 Superblock implementation: children racing on a track which was previously a street for motor traffic

set the right regulatory frameworks so that data and AI can be democratically controlled and managed as public infrastructures, as common good to create public value, build better services, and take accountable decisions.

As algorithmic decisions made by machines risk taking away the space for the exercise of human values, we need to look at the social, ethical, and economic implications of artificial intelligence and their impact on inclusion and inequality. In a world where artificial intelligence can reshape how wealth and power is distributed, it could discriminate against the most fragile people and accelerate polarization and inequalities. There is a need for an in-depth anthropological and ethical reflection to understand how AI shapes trust, power, truth, and knowledge. We need to protect human values and put human welfare at the center, shaping new alliances to forge a more humanistic future (Castellano Lubov 2023).

Only by coupling a digital transition with a Green New Deal will we be able to break the binary logic that always presents us with two scenarios for our digital future: Big State, the Chinese centralized and Orwellian model, or Big Tech, the Silicon Valley surveillance capitalism. Big State straps people of their individual liberties; Big Tech creates data monopolies that will eventually run critical infrastructure such as health care or education. Neither is an option for a democratic world. I advocate for a third way: Big Democracy. A democratization of data, citizen participation, and technology at the service of society and the ecological transition.

In the Age of the Anthropocene, we stand at a historical crossroads: we can take back our technological sovereignty, by advancing a new digital humanism that refuses Big State, Big Tech, and the Tech Wall between China and the US. In order to make this vision a reality, we need a new movement that can advance an alternative, making technology a right and an opportunity for people and the environment, and not a privilege for a few.

My suggestion is to start from a network of cities promoting ambitious policies to take back democratic governance of digital technology, data sovereignty, and green urban planning. This is the new social contract that we need in the digital society, where as a society we should be able to set the direction of technological progress and put technology and data at the service of people, human values, society, and the ecological transition. I am eager to engage in a conversation around how we take this vision beyond Europe, and how to make this vision a reality starting with concrete projects on the ground.

---

1 See page 39.

2 https://decodeproject.eu

3 https://citiesfordigitalrights.org

4 https://futureu.europa.eu/en

References

Bria, Francesca. 2018. "Our Data Is Valuable. Here's How We Can Take That Value Back." *Guardian*, April 5, 2018.

Castellano Lubov, Deborah. 2023. "Pope: AI Ethics Must Safeguard the Good of Human Family." *Vatican News*, January 10, 2023. www.vaticannews.va/en/pope/news/2023-01/pope-francis-receives-rome-call-vatican-audience.html.

Eggimann, Sven. 2022. "The Potential of Implementing Superblocks for Multifunctional Street Use in Cities." *Nature Sustainability* 5: 406–14. https://doi.org/10.1038/s41893-022-00855-2.

Zuboff, Shoshana. 2019. *The Age of Surveillance Capitalism: The Fight for a Human Future at the New Frontier of Power*. New York: Public Affairs.

9

how to build equity

Edgar Pieterse

Thank you for the invitation to be here. It has been a great privilege and learning experience. The topic that I was asked to speak to is how to build equity. I have reflected on Bjarke Ingels's and Francesca Bria's presentations since we're in the same slot. I think there is a hidden wisdom as to why that's the case. I ponder what that is. I am not entirely sure, because in some ways Francesca Bria's presentation was a critique of the environmental modernization that Bjarke Ingels represents through a compelling aesthetic register. Yet there is politics at the heart of those transitions, and we cannot ignore those politics, especially when we have a whole suite of new, so-called smart technologies that are difficult to contain.

What struck me, though, as [Francesca Bria] went through that whole panoply of EU charters, regulations, laws, et cetera, is how these EU projects do not extend in solidarity to the rest of the world. A good friend of mine, who led the trade negotiations between Africa and the EU, Carlos Lopez, stresses that if Europe unilaterally proceeds with carbon trade barriers before 2030, it directly reduces the scope and potential of Africa's economic development. This reminds us that there can be inconsistency between the internal conversation of the EU about rights, equity, and social justice, and how to imagine the instantiation of such public goods at a planetary scale, especially in regions such as Africa that are structurally marginalized in economic and political terms.

We are living through a series of extreme moments in history, of systemic and structural proportions, manifested as persistent and violent exclusion of one-third of the global population. We are living with those effects as a normalized reality. The question is, how do we think through that condition? What are the answers this particular initiative is trying to work through in this context? I begin with income and wealth distribution. As demonstrated in Figure 9.1, the top 10 percent of income earners aggregate a ridiculous amount of income and wealth around the world. According to the World Inequality Report 2022, if we look at average wealth growth between 1995 and 2021, the top 10 percent aggregate almost 40 percent of all global wealth growth (Chancel et al. 2022). This distributional pattern is at the heart of technological transitions and the emergence of

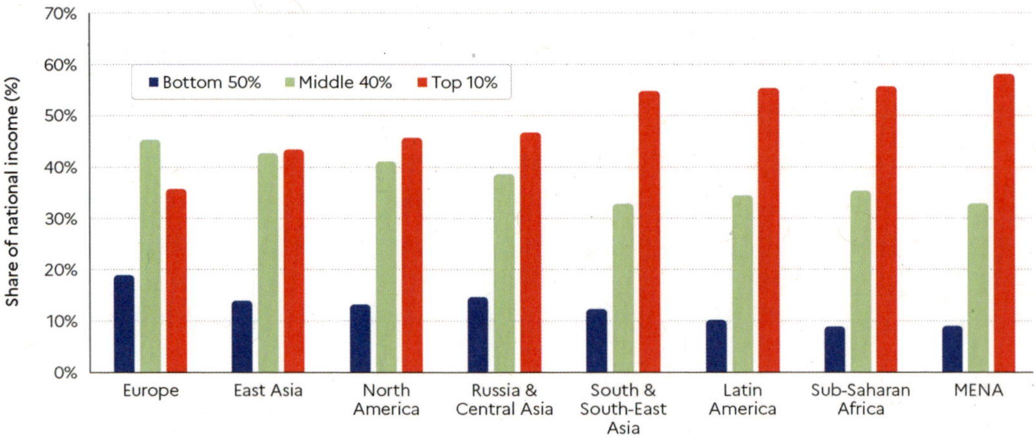

Fig. 9.1 Global income and wealth inequality, 2021

a sustainability consciousness. There is something deeply problematic in the translation of normative development frameworks into economic and political systems, institutions, and regulations.

I turn to Africa now and zoom in on thinking about equity at the neighborhood scale within a typical African city. It is important to recognize, as Bjarke Ingels does, that industrial modernity has delivered improvement in living standards, in education, health, household income, et cetera. However, in 2022, with an eye on the 2050 horizon, the future of work is profoundly uncertain. Therefore, when you look at the distribution of people in poverty, they live predominantly in sub-Saharan Africa. Based on the UN data, the labor force in Africa will treble between now and 2050, and currently 80 percent of urban employment is informal.

The reality of informal employment is less the issue. Rather, it is the fact that when you are in the informal economy, your income is extremely low and precarious. You cannot plan as a household; you cannot invest because you always have to anticipate profound dislocation or crises, whether it be inflationary increases or the effects of flooding or drought. Moreover, climate events in particular render people in informal employment most vulnerable. People are not just in informal jobs but are also living informally, in the midst of an explosive expansion of profound inequality. Evidence suggests that the structural drivers of exclusion are baked into the logics of the global economy, with reinforcing rules, especially the global trade and financial systems. Even if we know exactly what to do in technological terms to improve well-being, there are no easy answers about how to achieve such outcomes amidst systemic inequality because these are political questions, not merely technical.

If we connect the wealth distribution problem to those responsible for the carbon problem, we are back to the 10 percent. Figure 9.2 captures, by region, the share of the 10 percent that aggregates the bulk of wealth, and what their carbon contributions are. It is clear, if we want to talk about equity, the 10 percent is where we've got to start. However, I do not cover the 10 percent today; instead, I will speak about the 50 percent of the distribution that lives on the left-hand side of the graph, i.e., those who are not responsible for the climate crisis that the Bauhaus initiative is trying to resolve. Furthermore, if you look at the relatively insignificant contribution of SSA at a global scale, the same point applies. Be that as it may, because SSA is emblematic of the majority of the cities that I am interested in, I am curious about what is possible in those settings. Therefore, this is the context that the rest of my remarks refers to.

What do we mean by equity? For me, equity is not just about access to income, or enhanced livelihoods, or even the Sustainable Development Goals (SDGs). It is about three things: it resides within individuals in their social relationships, in their desire for meaning, and in their pleasure in life. There are countless routine social activities people do to achieve strong bonds, meaning, and pleasure. However, what the SDGs are interested in is the idea of security in a fundamental sense. The SDGs map neatly onto various capabilities in the sense that Amartya Sen defines. In fact, the SDGs are a successor to the Millennium Development Goals (MDGs) of 2000, which were the first attempt to codify and aggregate the capabilities frameworks. However, with the MDGs, we realized that we had not dealt with environmental externalities enough; and, more importantly, we had not dealt with inequality at all.

We now have two SDGs that deal with equality: SDG 5 on gender equality and SDG 10 on inequality at large. It is at the intersection of

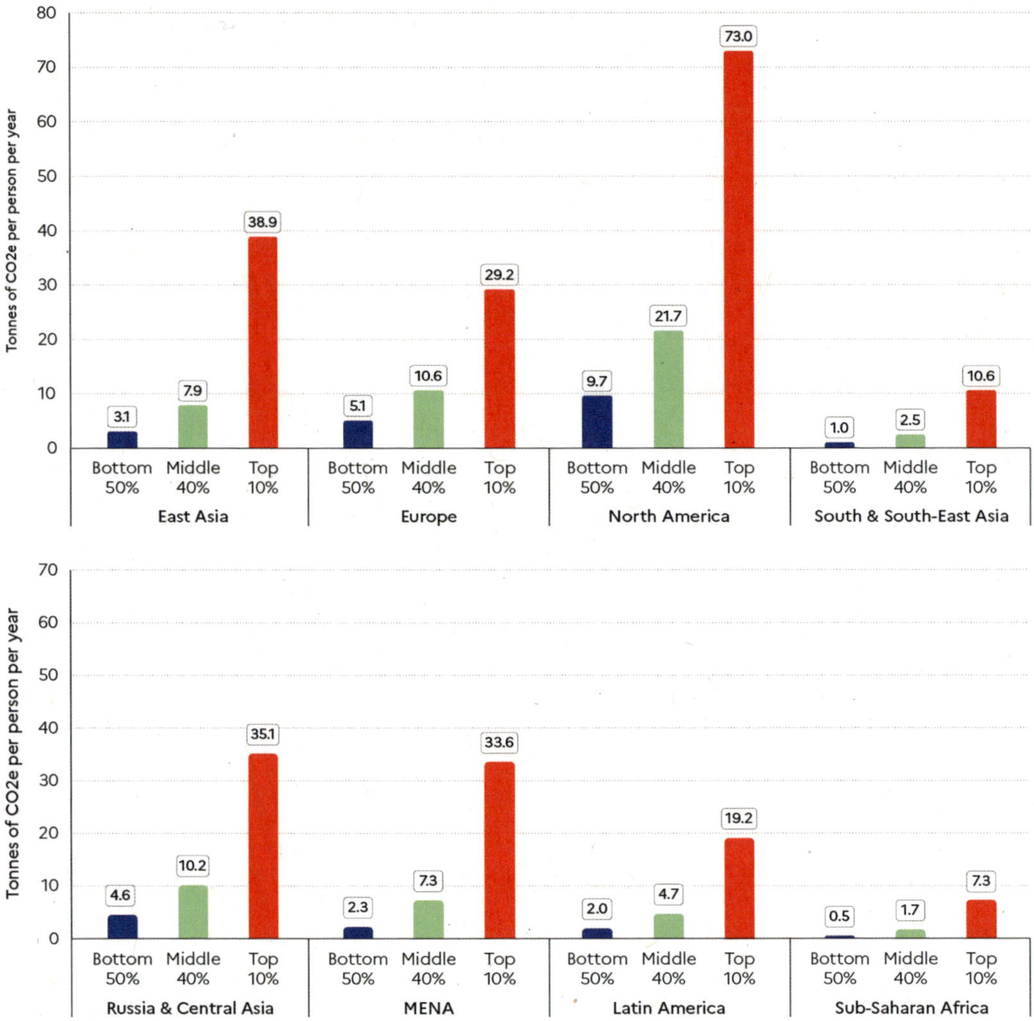

Fig. 9.2 Per capita emissions across the globe, 2019

foundational security, meaning, and pleasure-seeking practices that people find emotional attachment to place. This for me has got to be the ephemeral zone that should preoccupy our best thinking, experimentation, and so forth. However, the important thing to grasp is that belonging does not get delivered through physical infrastructure. Therefore, it is not just about achieving the SDGs; it is a much more complex dynamic. As Francesca Bria said earlier today, this is a governance project, this is a citizenship project, this is a participatory democracy imperative. The social-cultural elements that advance human flourishing is a topic that merits its own elaboration, but for now it is worthwhile figuring out how we blend it into our explorations; in particular, what it means to fundamentally rethink education, from early childhood development through to postgraduate education.

If our institutions are lagging, and our governance systems are lagging by 100 years in terms of where society is at, our educational institutions are probably lagging by 60 years. Therefore, there is great urgency to fundamentally rethink institutions, governance, and learning. As designers and urbanists, we may have a very simple question as our touchstone: Can we imagine what a life, a home, a street, a neighborhood might look and feel like if it is fundamentally based on expanding the capacity for love among children? What could that be? What if that is the only question we are trying to answer? Unfortunately, we have to go back to the bigger picture. What are the obstacles to inequality, and what is spatial inequality? Spatial inequality represents a materialization of these larger structural dynamics that shape places.

We see three main drivers of spatial inequality: (1) real estate market logics; (2) deeply entrenched cultural desires and imaginaries about the forms of late, informational modernity; (3) path-dependent dynamics rooted in colonial planning and systems of segregation. I draw your attention to them because even though there is an uptake in sustainability discourse, there is a greater increase in the reproduction of inequality, and that is because it is baked into the system. Real estate market logic drives urban development just about everywhere and is the backbone of the fiscal model at the city level. If you do not have an alternative source for financing infrastructure, it will be impossible to sustain necessary investments. The intimate relationship between real estate systems and urban governance is visible in the ways construction industries and property companies embed themselves in local governance systems by financing political parties and specific politicians—but that is a story for another day.

However, there exists another complicated issue, namely, the deeply entrenched desires imagined in forms of late, informational modernity that structure and drive aspiration. This means that the mere presentation of sustainable alternatives does not mean people and communities will find them acceptable or desirable.

African societies are also forced to deal with long-term processes of path dependency. African cities evolve through the legacies left by colonialism and extractive capitalism. This is part of the reason why rapid urbanization over the last 25 years on the continent is associated with urban sprawl marked by an ever-deepening dualism between classes, cultures, the built environment and nature, and definitely a reinforcement of systemic inequality and exclusion. The trends are crystal clear, yet this is at the same moment that we see an uptake in discourse and rhetoric that celebrates urban density, integration, and economic agglomeration without any reference to the material realities of sprawl and spatial inequality.

How might we build equity in that context? I cannot provide definitive answers to this question but hope the telling of three stories might intimate what it is we are searching for, and how we might systematize knowledge platforms that could articulate these experiments. I believe the Bauhaus der Erde initiative could be a very powerful generator of the collective learning infrastructure we need to fast-track learning. There is a whole set of components in these contexts around what I would call everyday dimensions of equity. There are the basics: access to infrastructure, water, energy, et cetera. Yet dignity is as important as a structuring variable of equity in any physical infrastructure and landscape.

Critically, in most African countries, administration, bureaucracy, and policy remains viciously arbitrary for the majority of urban dwellers who live in slums and work informally. People get exploited on a whim because police officers do not get paid properly. Therefore, an available form of accumulation is extortion by those who command some petty bureaucratic power. Today we had lots of debates, including on territorial concepts such as bioregionalism as a new scale for planning and collaboration, and metropolitan government as a way of aggregating fragmented local authorities to improve management. Then we have heard examples of the type of hyperlocalism that could only emerge in Barcelona and is harnessed through the superblock initiatives. Then we heard about the critical issue of interoperability, which enables seamless and transparent (at least that is the ambition and vision) articulations of data and information across these scales: bioregion, metropolitan administration, neighborhood, and street. Francesca Bria's presentation showed precisely the animation of data flows and metrics if you get it right. The Paris story about the 15-minute city, or the movements around 20-minute neighborhoods—that's all fine and well, but the real issue is the articulation of this at scale. The higher you go up the scale, the more depth you gain in reversing systemic power inequality if your interventions are sufficiently ambitious.

I finish with a focus on hyperlocalism. Much of the work on this is about trying to articulate three aspects: sustainable infrastructure; green building and, in the European context, the retrofit imperative, which demands a radically different frame for regulation; and institutional reform, which is lagging. However, there is a much more profound question. We cannot solve those issues until the philosophical disconnect between property regimes and ecosystem services is resolved. We have not done the philosophical work, we have not done the legal work, to reconcile these contradictory rationales; as a consequence, there is no framework to navigate everyday tensions in incentive and decision-making. The default is that private property regimes win out almost every time. Coming back to the point on land, made by Bjarke Ingels, it is the core problem. If there is a meta-question for me that this movement for sustainability in the built environment could animate, it would be to begin to bring brains together to address the disconnect between property regimes and ecosystem services. Until we resolve that, all the dangers we have heard of today are going to come to pass.

Formal economic jobs for the majority of the labor force in African cities are not likely in Africa due to the global division of labor surrounding industrialization, i.e., predominantly in China and Southeast Asia. For many low-income African countries that need to industrialize, the bus has already left the station. Therefore, we have to really think first from principles: How do we build an imaginary of local economies that can deal with large-scale unemployment and informal employment? What if we take all the various infrastructure systems in the city and the ideas we are trying to work through, around the circular and care economies, to their full potential in how we reimagine and construct cities, street by street? This approach requires aggregate forms of social enterprises and cooperative enterprises and a simultaneous move to rethink value chains of infrastructure sectors, the capital/labor ratio that is optimal in each sector so that all the discrete investments return to questions of equitable place-making. What we have found in our research is that, at the moment, there is no way the current financing systems can support this kind of approach even if there is political will. Very little of the green and climate finance hype goes far enough to advance alternative models in the political and institutional context of African cities. That is a massive disconnect.

Now I move on to case studies on place-making and alternative construction. [The project] nonCrete[1] is a social enterprise in Cape Town that conducts research and experiments in mainstream alternative construction in public housing and infrastructure value chains. They have developed a technique to reuse nonindigenous trees that overconsume scarce water resources as a feedstock for a robust construction material. It outperforms conventional brick and mortar by 1,000 percent according to studies done in conjunction with ETH Zurich. The main point is that it can all be done without machines, except for a wood chipper. The entire construction process is nonmechanical, and unskilled workers can be trained within days to become proficient in applying the construction technology. Despite considerable promise about the viability of the approach, numerous questions on how we would institutionalize this approach within government to underpin public housing and public infrastructure remain unanswered.

The second example is work on the informal condition as a lived reality in terms of homes, educational infrastructure such as creches, and public space, all of which are open to transformation through local labor and materials. During 2018/19 my organization, ACC, ran a design studio to develop a methodology to reenvision what an ecosystem of public infrastructure in deprived neighborhoods could

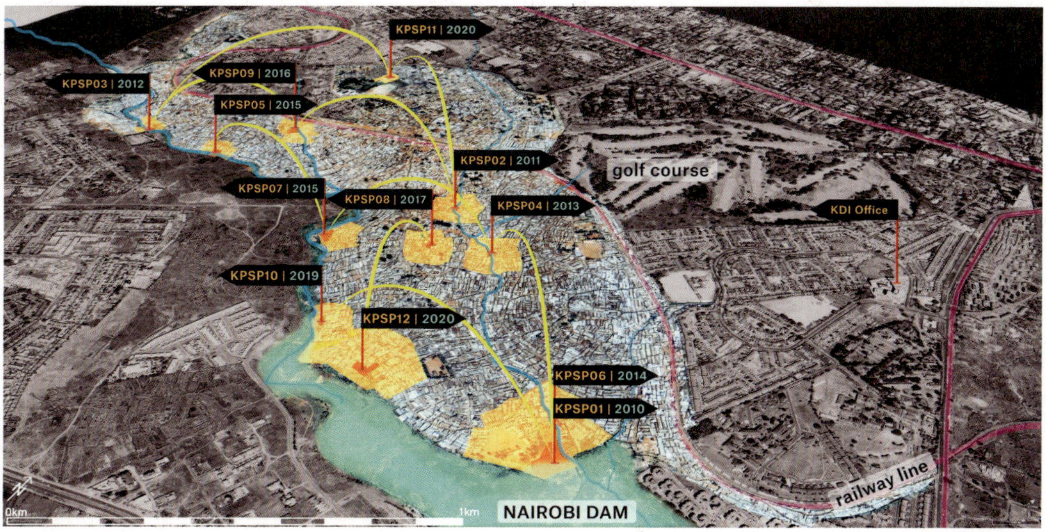

Fig. 9.3 KDI acupuncture sites across Kibera, Nairobi

look like and how best it can be optimized through local labor, aesthetics, and management (Pieterse et al. 2019). This outlook invites play and learning with beautifully adapted spaces.

My third example echoes this speculative approach but in the context of Kibera, a large informal settlement community in Nairobi, Kenya. The work is led by Kounkuey Design Initiative (KDI) and manifested as the Kibera Public Space Project.[2] KDI has built a fascinating framework for upgrading public infrastructure using green and blue infrastructures. Through this framework, they are able to activate community energy and knowledge, combined with design and engineering expertise, and are positioned to find support with the public sector and international partners. Tangible results have been produced in 12 acupuncture sites across Kibera, and Figure 9.4 demonstrates the kind of physical transformation these interventions are able to effect over time. The two pictures show the initial site covered in litter and waste that contaminated the adjacent dam, and how it was reclaimed and programmed as a multidimensional community resource.

This is one illustrative example of the transformation that is possible at the edge of the dam in Kibera. KDI has rolled out this approach across 12 public spaces using only local organizations, a

Fig. 9.4 KPSP site, before and after, Nairobi

local membership base, and local technologies, et cetera. The point is that this is what situated innovation enables. Today, we have seen quite a bit of systems thinking, quite a lot of design thinking, a lot of focus on technology, but there is no critical thought about historical path-dependent constraints that shape the power of place-making. We cannot afford such conceptual blind spots. Viable solutions will only emerge through participatory processes that solve problems in specific sites but are also aggregated through a set of frameworks that we can disseminate very quickly.

Thank you very much.

Sheela Patel From the morning, in our discussions on the New Bauhaus framework, I feel that we are talking only about the tip of the iceberg, which is the formal world. We have forgotten the Indigenous people, we have forgotten the informal people, we've forgotten landless agricultural workers. We have left one-third of humanity out of this discussion. The exclusion and the excitement of those beautiful visuals just reminds all of us that there is no clarity in our framework about what constitutes inclusion. I think from now onwards, however fabulous your presentations are, they must feel accountable. Just as you feel accountable to the planet, you have to feel accountable for one-third of the population that has been excluded for multiple generations. We are not doing that. So, Edgar, thank you, you've laid the outline for me, I do not have to say any of this tomorrow. Thank you.

Hans Joachim Schellnhuber Sheela, I'd like to make a comment. You are absolutely right, and you have been a champion of this debate for many years now. Indeed, in general, we talk about the problems of the wealthy part of the world population, the top billion, and we completely forget about the bottom billions, who live in Kibera as an example, and many of our informal settlements. The problem is that the top billion is creating conditions on earth that will destroy the globe for the entire population. That is the bitter irony of it. It makes sense if Europe and America try to stop the emissions of CO_2. We need to find a solution in Europe, the Global North, but we have to team up with the Global South. I ask this question: What if CO_2 were not a greenhouse gas? Still we would have misery all over the planet. If we are not able to solve the climate problem, then we will all be toast, all 10 billion of us.

Edgar Pieterse John,[3] on that, I completely get where you're coming from. What frustrates me is, why is reparations not on the agenda of the European Union? Why? Both in terms of slavery and in terms of climate. Secondly, apart from that, there is a redistributive question. If you look at what has happened to the debates on Official Development Assistance (ODA), and the 0.7 percent of GDP requirement established by the international community, it is evident that we are going backward, not forward (OECD, n.d.). Especially in the last 15 years, there has been this sleight of hand where trade-related investments are treated as ODA, which means there are even fewer resources for genuine developmental purposes. If we are talking about what I refer to as the 10 percent of wealth, in the distribution shown in Figure 9.1, or the top billion in your terms, then let us at least include these issues of reparations and redistribution in the agenda. If you do not have a mechanism to deal with the relationality between that 1 billion and the rest at a global scale, financially speaking, then we are nowhere.

1 https://noncrete.com/

2 www.kounkuey.org/projects/kibera_public_space_project_network

3 Edgar Pieterse is referring to Hans Joachim Schellnhuber.

References

Chancel, Lucas, Thomas Piketty, Emmanuel Saez, Gabriel Zucman, et al. 2021. *World Inequality Report 2022*. World Inequality Lab. https://wir2022.wid.world.

OECD. n.d. "The 0.7% ODA/GNI Target—A History." Accessed January 26, 2023. www.oecd.org/dac/financing-sustainable-development/development-finance-standards/the07odagnitarget-ahistory.htm.

Pieterse, E., P. Green, B. Knemeyer, A. Pulker, and A. Viviers, eds. 2019. *The Integration Syndicate: Shifting Cape Town's Socio-spatial Debate.* Cape Town: African Centre for Cities.

10

life, growth, and death: from organisms and cities to societies

Geoffrey West

Thank you. It's a great pleasure to be here, and I'm very flattered and honored to have been invited. I really enjoyed the sessions today. They're quite complementary to the way I think about cities and the planet, which is what I'm going to talk about. As you can see, the title is somewhat pretentious and grandiose, but it allows me to talk about almost anything. I'm going to give you a big-picture, hundred-thousand-meter-level of thinking about the planet and its potential future from a systemic, integrated view and in the spirit of what Bjarke [Ingels] was saying, but quite different, because I'm going to try to do science, since I'm a physicist.

I've spent my life doing fundamental physics and worked a lot on big questions of biology, and in more recent years I've tried to develop something known as the science of cities, trying to make a quantitative, predictive, computable analytic theory to understand the underlying mechanisms that might help us address the kinds of questions and challenges that we discuss here.

I'm going to begin with the words of John von Neumann, one of the great scientists of the 20th century, a mathematical physicist: "The ever accelerating progress of technology gives the appearance of approaching some essential singularity in the history of the race beyond which human affairs, as we know them, could not continue." It's remarkable that he said that nearly 70 years ago since it sounds so modern. What is also interesting about von Neumann is that almost everything he did, he mathematized. The amazing breadth of his work underlies why we use computers the way we do today, the foundations of quantum mechanics, economic theory, and the social sciences, including his invention of game theory, and much more. So it's quite surprising, even mysterious, why, when it came to the future of the planet, he never did anything mathematical beyond making this singular statement. So, in some very modest way, I'm going to try to put some flesh on the bones of those words, and I'm going to do it by first showing you something that you're extremely familiar with. It's been mentioned in some of the talks, but no one has actually shown it explicitly.

It's a plot of the population growth of the world over the last 12,000 years. What you see is that after a gradual but continuous increase for the first 11,000 years or so, there was a sharp, almost discontinuous, increase in population beginning near the end of the 18th century, driven, as you well know, by the Industrial Revolution. This was when we discovered fossil fuels, learned how to exploit them, and, at the same time, developed entrepreneurship, capitalism, and free markets. Together, these led us to this extraordinary world we live in today. In terms of conventional standards of living, all of us, and especially those of us in the developed world, have benefited enormously from this.

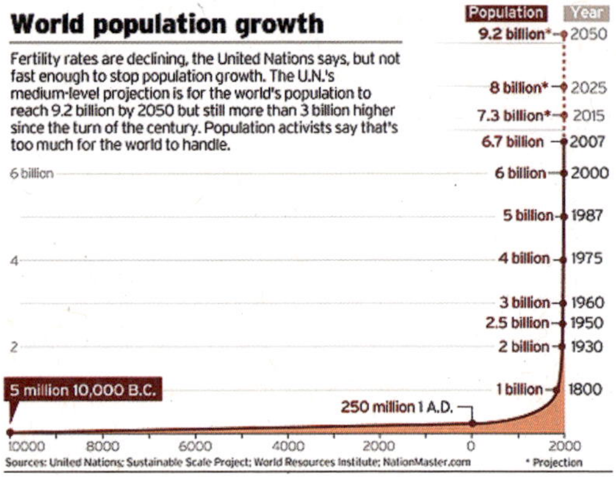

Fig. 10.1 12,000 years of population growth

Since this major transition, the population has risen almost vertically on this scale, appearing to lead, in the words of von Neumann, to a singularity. In fact, even though everybody knows we live in an exponentially expanding physical universe, most people don't realize we also actually live in a faster than exponential socioeconomic universe. To illustrate this, here's a picture that I have concocted of what I imagine a NASA satellite photo of the earth at night would have looked like in the year I was born, 1940, compared with what it looks like today. Those lights are the night lights of cities and the change represents the astonishing rate at which we have urbanized the planet.

Fig. 10.2 Earth the year I was born and now

Fig. 10.3 How we image cities (left)

Fig. 10.4 What a city really is, without its buildings (right)

That is pretty extraordinary given the short period of time—one old man's lifetime—during which this has happened. But what this really represents—you know what it is—is the earth literally burning up because what you're seeing as night lights of cities—almost all of that energy—is driven by the burning of fossil fuels. The surface of the planet is burning and it's burning faster and faster, and only a thoughtless person could believe that does not affect the climate or warm the globe.

Now, what does this mean in numbers? From now to mid-century, we're urbanizing on average over a million people a week, maybe it's 2 million. That's equivalent to adding a New York metropolitan area every few months, or a country the size of Denmark every few days, or a Germany every year. That's what we're doing now.

When we think of a city, we usually conjure up an image like that in Figure 10.3—its buildings, roads, electrical lines, and so forth. We view it in terms of its built environment, its physicality and infrastructure. This is what a city is, but it's much more than that. All of those buildings are just a stage, a backdrop, for facilitating social interaction. Cities are the most powerful machines we've ever invented because they facilitate social interactions that increase innovation, wealth production, and the creation of ideas, and, consequently, the standard and quality of life for all citizens. That's why cities are so attractive. So, a more realistic image of a city is that shown in Figure 10.4, where we viscerally feel the buzz and potential of social interaction being facilitated by the physical built environment. Great cities have multiple venues to enhance this dynamic: public squares and plazas, lecture and concert halls, sports stadia, offices, coffee houses, et cetera, et cetera—all designed to bring people together and create!

In that picture, A talks to B, B talks to C, C talks to D, and they talk back and forth to one another. We build on what each other is saying, continuously creating ideas, almost all of which are useless and pointless to anybody else. But what's amazing is that every once in a while, in the spirit of what's happening in that picture, this dynamic produces a theory of relativity or quantum mechanics, or a Google or a General Motors, or the Vatican. How does that all happen? It happens through the positive feedback inherent in social networks, building on what's been said before. Networks, both social and infrastructural (roads, electrical, gas, water lines, et cetera), underlie the structure and dynamics of cities.

Generally speaking, all these networks have approximately the same geometric pattern: they're typically hierarchical, branching, and fractal-like, much like a tree. Urban networks look like the networks inside you that keep you alive. In fact, they're actually very similar, except you're three-dimensional whereas a city tends to be two-dimensional. Biology is replete with such networks.

What is fascinating about biological networks is that their mathematics and physics lead to something quite surprising, namely, systematic scaling laws. You usually think of natural selection in terms of organisms evolving arbitrarily and capriciously in their own unique environmental niches and fundamentally being historically contingent. But the network theory predicts that if you look at metabolic rate, for instance, how much food you need each day to stay alive, and you plot it versus size for a series of animals, you should see something extremely simple and systematic, despite its extraordinary complexity. Plotting it logarithmically is predicted to reveal a simple straight line, completely antithetical to the idea that it's arbitrary and capricious, in which case the points would be spread over the graph.

These are fundamental laws that constrain every part of every organism. The slope of the line is predicted by the mathematical theory to be 3/4, as observed (Figure 10.5). In fact, it predicts that if you plot almost anything that you can measure about life, logarithmically against size from the microscopic up to ecosystems, whether

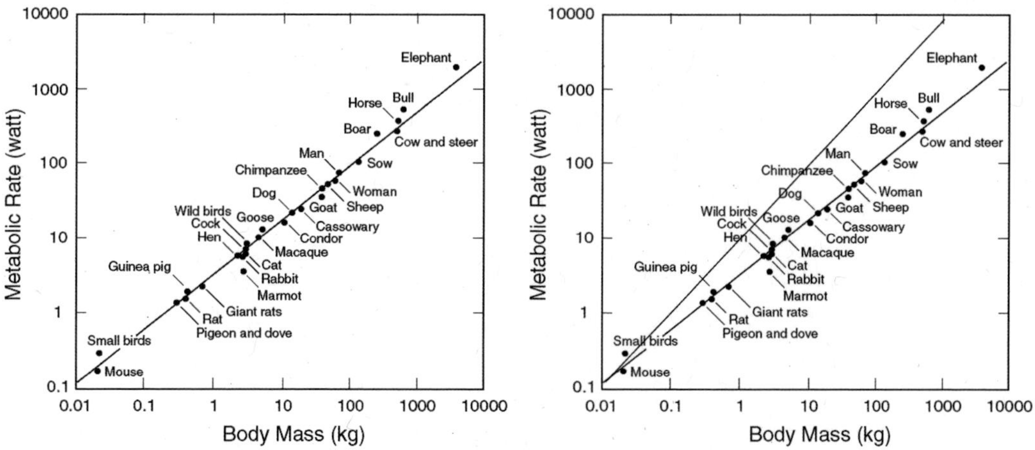

Fig. 10.5 Metabolic rates vs. natural selection

physiological or life history, it should be a straight line whose slope is a simple multiple of 1/4. There are more than 50 such scaling laws. The magic number four controls all of life, a fact everyone should know.

Naively, you might have expected the scaling to be linear, a slope of 1: double the size, you double the number of cells, and therefore double the amount of food you need. No, you (meaning every mammal) are very economic. The scaling law says that every time you double your size, you save about 25 percent in energy use. The bigger you are, the more efficient you are, and this has enormous implications across the entire biosphere. I'm just going to show you one example of this.

Fig. 10.6 Economy of scale in metabolic energy

I'm going to talk about growth because that's fundamental to everything. How do you grow? You eat, you metabolize, you send metabolic energy through the network. It goes partially to maintain what's there, repairs damage to cells, and partially to grow new ones; and you can put this into a mathematical equation. The incoming metabolic energy scales sublinearly. It's got an economy of scale, so less is needed per cell as the organism grows. That's the supply, but the demand increases linearly as cells are added, increasing faster than the supply because you're adding cells at a linear rate. Consequently, you

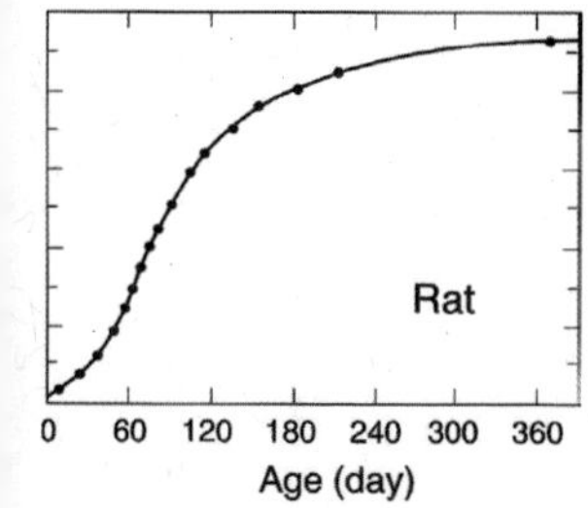

eventually stop growing, and that's why your growth curve looks sigmoidal, like in Figure 10.6. You don't need genes to make it happen—it's guaranteed by the network dynamics. This explains why you can eat large amounts of food each day, but guess what? Once you're mature, you no longer grow ontogenetically.

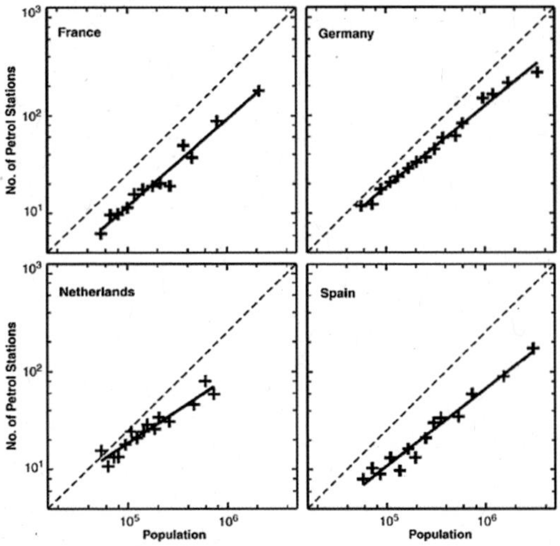

Fig. 10.7 Number of petrol stations compared to population size

Okay, so these are hidden laws of biology. I'd love to show you more of them because they're so fascinating and beautiful, revealing the amazing, almost spiritual, interrelationship and connectedness of all life around you. Instead, I'm going to ask whether there are similar laws for human-made systems such as cities, companies, or universities?

I'm only going to talk about cities here, and the answer is yes. For instance, this is the number of petrol stations plotted logarithmically versus city size, and you see again a systematic behavior as in biology (Figure 10.7). The only difference is that the slope is about 0.85 rather than 0.75. The dotted lines are linear, so the scaling is sublinear, indicating an economy of scale. The bigger you are, the fewer gas stations you need per capita. This is just for four European countries and they all look the same. What is fascinating is that across the globe, in Latin America, China, Japan, et cetera, urban systems behave exactly like this for gas stations, but guess what? They look like that for all infrastructure, whether buildings, roads, electrical lines, water lines, et cetera. All infrastructure scales similarly across the globe, manifesting an economy scale with a 15 percent savings with each doubling, rather than the 25 percent in biology.

That suggests that the entropy produced by energy use (pollution, carbon, and general disorder) should also manifest an economy of scale. A side comment: as a physicist, it's a bit disappointing that the word *entropy* has not been used yet in this meeting, because that's really what we're talking about when addressing problems from inequality to the degradation of the environment. Here's one:

the carbon emissions in cities. As predicted, this scales sublinearly, which means the bigger the city, the less carbon produced per capita. Much greener to be in New York than Santa Fe, where I live. Bigger cities are systematically greener in this technical sense than smaller cities.

Well, that's the less interesting part of cities, the infrastructure, the physical. The more interesting part is you and me, our social networks and interactions. The city is the integration between information exchange in social networks and its infrastructural networks (its "biology"). Infrastructure typically has a very different timescale than these information systems. Infrastructure could be there for hundreds of years, but people are born and die, come and go, interacting over much shorter timescales, while the same basic dynamic continues. People get replaced, while infrastructure typically persists, and the system evolves through continuous innovations.

Okay, so there it is. The positive feedback in social networks that leads to scaling originates in similar sorts of networks as in biology except it's information being exchanged instead of energy and resources. This latter case leads to sublinear scaling and economies of scale (the bigger you are, the less per capita) and to the cessation of growth, which underlies stability and sustainability and why life has been around for several billion years. For cities, we find superlinear scaling with a common slope of about 1.15 (Figure 10.8): instead of the bigger you are, the less per capita, it's the bigger you are, the more per capita (by about 15 percent with each doubling), and instead of

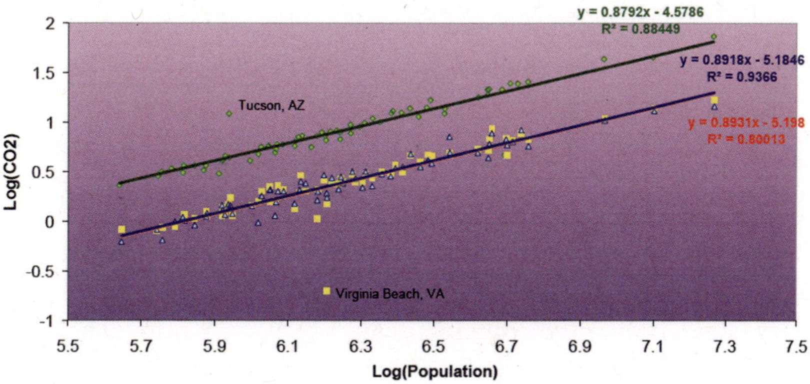

Fig. 10.8 The bigger you are, the more per capita

the pace of life slowing down as you increase in size, the pace of life increases; and all of this comes out of the mathematics of networks.

The scaling laws for the many very different socioeconomic metrics in different countries all look surprisingly similar, and we know why. They all originate from social interactions, and these are pretty much the same across the globe. After all, we're all human beings with essentially the same genes and histories. This also shows you that all the apparently different metrics are interconnected both between themselves and across the globe. If you mess with one system, if you try to mitigate a problem in one place without thinking of it systemically, you're very likely to induce unintended consequences somewhere else. The pandemic is a marvelous case of that. Who would think that an arbitrary mutation of a virus in Wuhan, China, would result in no flour in the United States, that Hertz would go bankrupt, or that there'd be no football in Spain, and much more. And all within a few months! Who would have ever thought they were connected? You know something? They were always connected, even if only very weakly. They're connected now, they were connected before, and they're going to be connected in the future, and if you only focus on one problem in one place, you are not going to solve the big problem. We need to act on all those problems in an integrated, holistic fashion, which requires a big-picture framework.

To summarize the scaling results: on average, if you double the size of a city, you systematically save approximately 15 percent on all infrastructure and therefore on some of the bad things that result from it, and at the same time, you increase social interactions by about 15 percent and therefore the good things such as income, wealth, ideas, patents, and education, but also the bad and ugly, such as crime and disease.

There's much more to talk about, but I'm going to finish up very quickly by considering the planet as a whole. I want to explore whether we could derive an equation for the entire planet! Whimsically, I call it a Master Anthropocene Equation: the beginnings of a systemic theory of sustainability. Here's the picture that John[1] showed earlier of the time development of various planetary metrics, which all look like hockey sticks, reflecting the superexponential increase in population (Figure 10.9). This is sometimes referred to as the Great Acceleration. Well, I'm going to translate these into scaling relationships, focusing on three of the obvious ones: energy, GDP, and water plotted versus population size. As you see, they do indeed scale, and much like cities, they do it superlinearly.

You can understand these in a similar way that we understood the growth of organisms as driven by metabolic rate. John already referred to social metabolic rate, the metabolic rate of the whole planet. As before, this gets apportioned between maintenance of what's already there (every person, institution, every road and building, all the infrastructure) and new growth (the addition of new versions of all these, from people, ideas, and institutions to buildings, artifacts, and so on). When you express this mathematically, it's quite daunting and pretty awesome, but you can do it and, amazingly, in an average sense, you can solve the equations.

Before discussing their solution, I want to say something about your metabolic rate. Just sitting here patiently waiting for me to finish my overly long talk, it's only about 100 watts, which is the 2,000 food calories you eat a day. Remarkably, you only need the energy of a light

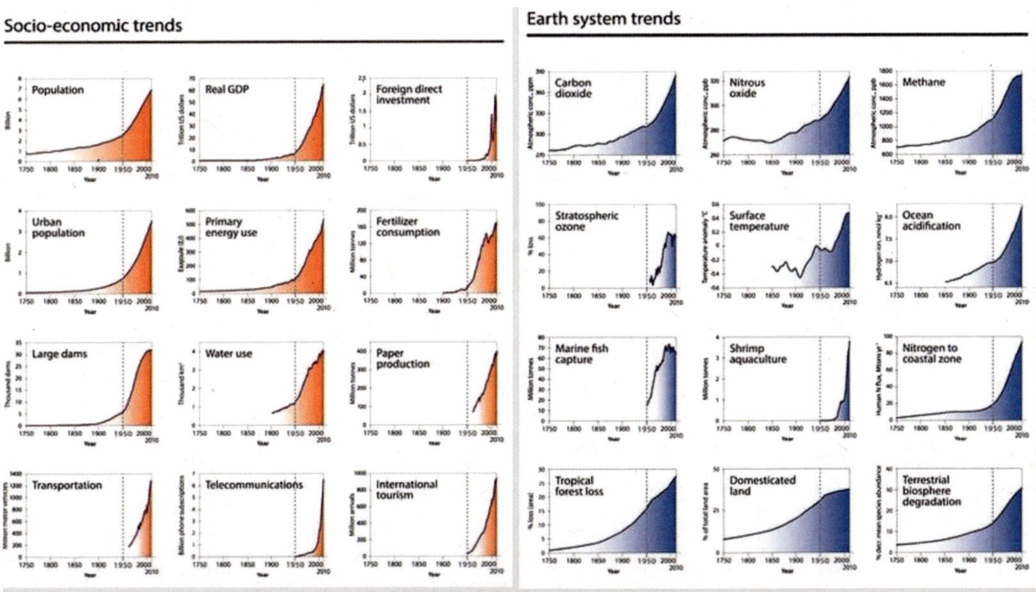

Updated Great Acceleration Graphs

Source: Will Steffen et al. "The trajectory of the Anthropocene: The Great Acceleration." The Anthropocene Review, March 2015

Fig. 10.9 The Great Acceleration

bulb to stay alive! You are incredibly efficient. However, your social metabolic rate, which includes all the energy you need to sustain your active lifestyle—lights, a car, a house, refrigerator, et cetera, et cetera—adds up to about 11,000 watts, 100 times bigger. When we were pre-urban hunter-gatherers, this active metabolic rate was only 200 to 300 watts! We are now extremely profligate and very inefficient. Here's the metabolic rate graph again (Figure 10.5). That's how we evolved. We fit exactly where we should with the right metabolic rate for our size. We also have the right length of our aorta, the right diffusion rate of oxygen for our lungs, and so on. We were in harmony with the entire biosphere. But this is where we are now (Figure 10.10). We've gone way up by a factor of 100 and you can ask how big an animal are we really? Each one of us in this room behaves as if they weighed about 30,000 kilograms in terms of what we are doing on this planet, equivalent to about a dozen elephants!

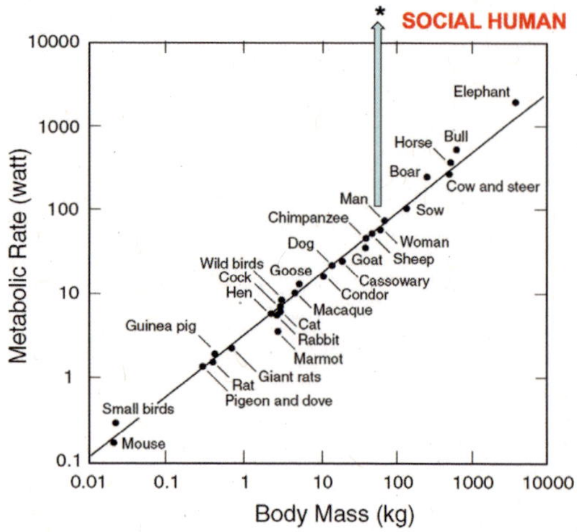

Fig. 10.10 Where we are now, in terms of metabolic rates

Recall that the growth curve based on sublinear scaling leads to a finite size, stability, and sustainability. Superlinear scaling, however, leads to open-ended growth, the foundation of modern economies. This is great because it's predicted by the theory as originating in the positive feedback dynamics in social networks that leads to superlinear scaling, and this leads to open-ended growth. So this is very satisfying. It explains the data, which is wonderful, but it also has built into it a potentially dire consequence, something called a finite time singularity (the vertical dotted line at t_c). This says that in some finite time in the future, it could be next year, it could be in five years or 50 years, key socioeconomic metrics will become infinite, which is obviously crazy. But the theory tells you what happens. It says that, if there are no major changes or interventions, the system will collapse beyond the singularity. How do you avoid that? You avoid it by making major changes, a major innovation or paradigm shift, effectively reinventing yourself and resetting the clock. And we've done that brilliantly. We had the Stone Age, the Bronze and Iron

Ages, we discovered coal and capitalism, we invented the computer and, most recently, IT, and the internet. Each of these set a new defining paradigm that dominated that age.

So, to sustain open-ended growth you have to make a major paradigm shift or innovation. But this only postpones the problem, it doesn't solve it. The same inextricable underlying social dynamics continue, and you're destined to hit another singularity. This leads to a sort of theorem: if you demand unbounded growth, you have to have continuous cycles of innovation and they have to come faster and faster in a systematic, predictable way.

The theory predicts where that singularity is, and gives the equation for how you approach that singularity: if you make a logarithmic plot of any key socioeconomic metric versus the time to the next singularity, then you should see straight lines with predictable slopes. Remarkably, this is confirmed by the data, as you can see. We're heading for a singularity, whether we like it or not. That's what the data is telling us.

We'd better do something about it, and very quickly! We are like Sisyphus, condemned to pushing the great boulder up the hill, where it rolls down again, but each time, unlike Sisyphus, we have to push it up faster and faster. The question is, how sustainable is that and how do we intervene to stop it? That's what von Neumann was warning us about. Fundamentally, it's all to do with social interactions and cities, so ultimately it very likely requires an innovation beyond technology, maybe the greatest of all paradigm shifts, namely, fundamental social and cultural change.

1 Geoffrey West is referring to Hans Joachim Schellnhuber.

→

11

regulations for the future

Klaus Mindrup

I was a member of the German Bundestag from 2013 to 2021. The most important task of a member of Parliament is to ensure good legislation. I am an ecologist and not a lawyer. But it is precisely this view of the non-lawyer that is important when drafting legislation.

In my presentation, I will focus on fossil carbon dioxide emissions as the most significant greenhouse gas. I will speak to the European and German perspective.

Good rules should motivate. As Antoine de Saint-Exupéry (1900–1944) said, "If you want to build a ship, don't drum up people to collect wood and don't assign them tasks and work, but rather teach them to long for the endless immensity of the sea."

We are all gathered here in Rome because we want a world in which we, as human beings, once again live in harmony with the earth and the climate, thus creating the conditions for future generations to have a good life on this earth. Can there be a greater motivation for good regulation?

Good regulation demands respect. Good climate protection regulation must have the most vulnerable people and ecosystems as well as future generations in mind.

I was there in person when the Paris Agreement was adopted on December 12, 2015, at the UN Climate Change Conference in Paris (COP 21). This agreement, and above all the goal of limiting man-made global warming to well below 2°C compared with preindustrial levels, represents an outstanding step forward in human history.

Since the Paris Agreement is an agreement between states, including the EU, it is logical that state borders play a decisive role. This is also the reason for the source principle anchored in the agreement. Emissions are accounted for in the countries where they occur. Nationally Determined Contributions (NDCs) define the Paris Agreement and the achievement of its long-term goals (UNFCCC, n.d.). These embody the efforts of individual countries to reduce national emissions and adapt to the impacts of climate change.

Fig. 11.1 Parking lot superstructure with a timber hybrid building, Dantebad, Munich

This leads to effects that need to be known. For example, Germany exported large amounts of electricity to France in 2021 and also in 2022 (Statista Research Department 2022). The cause was and is massive operational failures of French nuclear power plants (Schneider et al. 2022). In order to export to France, fossil fuel power plants had to be commissioned in Germany that would otherwise not have been used. This is the main reason why emissions from electricity generation in Germany have risen. The emissions are accounted for in Germany, although the cause is not in Germany. This rule and this cause-effect relationship apply in principle to all imports and exports across national borders.

Since both shipping and air transport largely pass through international waters or over international territories, the associated emissions cannot be attributed to any state (BMWK, n.d.). Shipping emissions are a major driver of man-made climate change (Ritchie 2020) that is not adequately reflected in government statistics.

The sole application of the source principle also leads to a distorted perception for the building sector. According to the current calculation methods in Germany, only 16.2 percent of the emissions of fossil CO_2 equivalent are attributable to the building sector (Umweltbundesamt 2022). In Germany, these are mainly the emissions from heating buildings. However, if one considers the entire life cycle, from the production of the building materials, their transport, operation, and finally the disposal of the buildings, emissions attributable to buildings over their entire life cycle account for approximately 40 percent of greenhouse gas emissions worldwide. In Germany, the figure would be of a similar order of magnitude.

In order to achieve effective regulation, we must therefore broaden our perspectives and not make the source principle alone the yardstick for our actions.

The "polluter pays" principle and life cycle analysis are the better basis for effective and goal-oriented action and should also be implemented at the state level on an equal footing with the source principle (von Kittlitz 2022).

The Greenhouse Gas Protocol[1] offers good approaches. In particular, accounting separately for Scope 1 (all direct emissions, i.e., those from sources within the boundaries), Scope 2 (which includes indirect emissions from externally generated and purchased electricity, steam, heating, and cooling), and Scope 3 (all other indirect emissions, including those from the production and transport of purchased goods, or distribution and use of the company's own products or the disposal of waste; also emissions due to business travel) is purposeful.

For the building sector, this holistic approach leads to sensible measures, which, however, have to be assigned to different sectors of the German Climate Protection Act.

The use of biological materials such as wood, hemp, or bamboo is to be assigned to the industry sector in the source accounting. The production of electricity on and at the building through PV and small wind as well as decentralized storage are to be assigned to the energy sector. New mixed districts with residential, commercial, and leisure facilities reduce the volume of traffic and thus emissions in the transport sector. The production of food on roofs and in neighborhood gardens is a climate-friendly variant in the agriculture sector.

This list shows the potential for climate protection that arises when a targeted approach and regulation is oriented toward the decision-makers and not toward theoretically chosen responsibilities.

This target-oriented approach is also urgently needed in view of the dramatic climate crisis.

The climate crisis also requires a realignment of goals. Until now, climate neutrality has been considered the necessary goal. However, according to the current state of science, this goal is not sufficient to stop dramatic climate change. According to the IPCC, negative emissions are necessary for this, as [Hans Joachim] Schellnhuber also emphasized in his opening speech today.[2] This means that we need to become "climate positive," and the building sector can play a key role in this through the long-term use of biological materials. Materials from biological sources such as wood, hemp, or bamboo store carbon dioxide and fulfill the criterion of being climate positive. The larger their share in the built environment becomes, the better for climate protection. We therefore need to make climate-positive materials from biological sources a clear priority. In this way, buildings and later entire city districts can become climate positive. This makes much more sense than burning biological materials and then injecting carbon emissions underground, as with carbon capture and storage (CCS).

Of course, these biological materials must come from sustainable production and must in no way endanger the protection of species and biotopes, and must therefore not damage primary forests, for example.

However, current regulations do not yet go far enough in this direction. Common regulations and incentives are CO_2 pricing, building regulations, public procurement, public financing, taxation, grants, and loans.

I would like to take CO_2 pricing as an example. In Germany, we have a coexistence of the ETS/European Emissions Trading Scheme (power plants, industry, and aviation) under the responsibility of the

EU and the national fuel emissions trading scheme for the sectors under national responsibility.

I negotiated the national system as a member of Parliament in the legislative process. We have introduced a system that will work like the European emissions trading system after 2027. Only as many CO_2 emission rights will then be auctioned as are permissible under the national climate protection law. This will lead to significant cost increases for all combustion processes using fossil fuels such as oil or natural gas and ensure that the targets of the national climate protection law are met.

Since CO_2 pricing systems around the world work in such a way that government revenues lead to expenditures elsewhere, there is a risk that people will "get used" to the revenues and thus to the CO_2 emissions, which would not be a good development in view of the worsening climate crisis. If you build a system of dependence on these revenues, we will find it difficult to stop emissions. CO_2 pricing is therefore a complicated scheme and not a panacea for solving all climate change challenges. It makes sense, but it is not a silver bullet.

According to the current German climate protection law, all fossil fuels will be banned from 2045. CO_2 pricing will therefore come to

Fig. 11.2 Three-floor extension on a WBS 70,[3] prefabricated building in timber hybrid construction, Berlin

an end by then at the latest, because if we stop burning fossil fuels, it will no longer be needed. CO_2 pricing is therefore only a bridge to the ban. That is why alternatives to it should already be in development now.

This is also necessary because, among other things, there are currently exemptions and reductions for CO_2 emissions from industry in the EU, so that, for example, building materials are protected from competition from outside the EU. However, this regulation puts building materials from biological sources such as wood at a disadvantage within the EU compared with steel, concrete, clinker, and insulation materials from fossil sources. Wood and other biological materials are not treated fairly here. The EU wants to solve this problem by removing the exemptions from CO_2 pricing combined with a CO_2 border adjustment (CBAM) at the EU's external borders. It remains to be seen whether this is possible under world trade law, and corresponding lawsuits are to be expected.

At the same time, there are other strategies that could well be followed and which could certainly be pursued in a complementary manner.

Ironically, we can learn from the regulation of the automotive sector, among others. If you visit the General Motors (GM) museum in Detroit, you can see electric vehicles that are 130 years old. Electric motors are much more efficient than internal combustion engines, but they did not catch on because the internal combustion vehicle was more convenient to use after the invention of petrol stations. Only the development of modern batteries combined with fleet regulation, introduced in California and adapted in Europe, has revived electric vehicles in modern form. Now, due to government regulation, every car manufacturer has to invest in batteries, electric cars, and electric motors, and the end of the combustion engine has been decided in the EU.

In addition to fleet regulation for cars, we can also learn from the German Renewable Energy Sources Act, which started in 2000. First, it made investments in renewable energies in the electricity

Fig. 11.3 New wooden building for cooperative housing, Ostseeplatz eG, Berlin

sector possible with the feed-in tariff. Second, it contains a clear path, a clear target orientation toward 100 percent renewable electricity. This triggered innovations worldwide in the use of wind and solar power for electricity generation, with dramatic cost reductions.

But what can we learn from these examples?

More climate-friendly technologies need good regulation, a commercially viable market introduction, and thus the emergence of alternatives. Once these alternatives are there, they must be clearly favored over the climate-damaging alternatives, which unfortunately is rarely the case.

In the building sector, many climate-friendly alternatives already exist and more will develop.

I am an active housing cooperative member and it is the cooperatives that are particularly innovative because they know that new housing is needed in view of population trends. At the same time, cooperatives are very long-term and oriented toward providing for several generations. That is why they often also have planetary boundaries and future generations in mind.

Good pilot projects in cooperative housing construction with wood have been developed in Berlin and Munich. This development is closely linked to the innovative German *Mittelstand* as manufacturers. It is also relevant that timber construction is not only climate friendly but also particularly suitable for serial production, which is effective and urgently needed in view of the lack of housing in many parts of Germany.

Why not take this approach further and introduce a climate-positive law with a clear prioritization of materials and value chains from biological sources?

In the building sector, this can be accompanied by clear regulation over the entire life cycle, according to which buildings must become climate positive step by step over the next few years. It is not a law of nature that only the energy consumption of buildings, appliances, or vehicles may be regulated. This regulation can and should then also integrate circularity (cradle-to-cradle).

This type of regulation has the advantage that, as already described for the building sector, it has an immediate effect across all sectors and in the supply chains, because it starts directly with the actors involved. Regionalized production then automatically has an advantage over imports from a great distance; today, it is rather the other way round. In parallel, the pressure for production changes and environmentally friendly transport is increasing worldwide, and at the same time the economic basis for new climate-friendly production and innovations is laid.

Climate protection thus becomes a win-win situation. Local and climate-friendly production is promoted. Climate-positive buildings will achieve a higher level of acceptance than the alternatives made of steel and concrete, and thus help to make progress in the necessary housing construction.

This approach can be applied worldwide. It still requires a lot of work on the details. However, because of its clear goal orientation, it has a greater chance of being effective than the current, often bureaucratic approaches, which are full of loopholes due to the successful lobbying of the lawyers for the old fossil industries.

The future for people and the planet makes it worth fighting for climate-positive cities and villages.

---

1 https://ghgprotocol.org/

2 See page 30.

3 Type of dwelling built in the German Democratic Republic using slab construction. It was developed in the early 1970s by the German Academy of Architecture and the Technical University of Dresden.

References

BMWK (Bundesministerium für Wirtschaft und Klimaschutz). n.d. *Luftverkehr und Schifffahrt.* Accessed January 27, 2023. www.carbon-mechanisms.de/grundlagen/grundlagen-der-kohlenstoffmaerkte/luftverkehr-und-schifffahrt.

Ritchie, Hannah. 2020. "Sector by Sector: Where Do Global Greenhouse Gas Emissions Come From?" *Our World in Data*, September 18, 2020. https://ourworldindata.org/ghg-emissions-by-sector.

Schneider, Mycle, Antony Froggatt, Julie Hazemann, Christian von Hirschhausen, M.V. Ramana, Alexander James Wimmers, Michael Sailer, et al. 2022. *The World Nuclear Industry Status Report 2022.* A Mycle Schneider Consulting Project. www.worldnuclearreport.org/IMG/pdf/wnisr2022-v3-lr.pdf.

Statista Research Department. 2022. "Menge des exportierten Stroms von Deutschland nach Frankreich in den Jahren 2003 bis 2022." *Statista*, August 9, 2022. https://de.statista.com/statistik/daten/studie/151340/umfrage/strom-export-von-deutschland-nach-frankreich-seit-1996/.

Umweltbundesamt. 2022. "Energiesparende Gebäude." *Umweltbundesamt*, June 3, 2022. www.umweltbundesamt.de/themen/klima-energie/energiesparen/energiesparende-gebaeude#gebaude-wichtig-fur-den-klimaschutz.

UNFCCC. n.d. "Nationally Determined Contributions (NDCs): The Paris Agreement and NDCs." *UNFCCC*. Accessed January 27, 2023. https://unfccc.int/ndc-information/nationally-determined-contributions-ndcs.

von Kittlitz, Valerie. 2022. "Warum wir jetzt keinen Mist bauen dürfen." *Deutschlandfunk Kultur*, March 1, 2022. www.deutschlandfunkkultur.de/neubau-klimaziele-nachaltigkeit-bezahlbares-wohnen-100.html.

12

50 years since *the limits to growth*: learning to live within limits

Sandrine Dixson-Declève

I want to move into the important [From Mining to Gardening] session, as we look at the shift behind the scenes in how we create the societal fabric of our cities, and the interrelationship with the Anthropocene.

I am hearing from all of you that one key aspect of this societal fabric of urban areas that we need to address is the importance of systems. How do we properly acknowledge the role of systems and the need for systems transformation? Obviously, coming from the Club of Rome, systems change, and the interrelationships between systems have been core to our thinking for the last 50 years.

In this 50th-anniversary year of the publication of the seminal report *The Limits to Growth*, we are reminded that *The Limits to Growth* was already talking about urgency 50 years ago, and the fact that the alarm bells were ringing as the global population was growing, and extractive societies were pushing the planetary boundaries to the limit of what was possible for humanity to thrive, not just survive as we see today. This idea of thriving is fundamental.

As we look at the findings of the Club of Rome over the last 50 years, in particular the great systems thinking of Donella Meadows, and her work on leverage points for change within systems, we already have most of the solutions for today's wicked problems and a great compass for action. The starting point is addressing the connectivity between the social system, the economic system, the global commons, and the political system in the midst of chaos and in the midst of what I call the compound effect of the three Cs—climate change, COVID-19, and conflict—which are all three on our doorstep. This is the first signal of a permanent state of crisis, now referred to as a perma-crisis. How do we best apply the leverage points and systems thinking when we know that the impacts of growth and overconsumption are the cause of the three Cs—population growth and the shift in demographics, the overuse of our natural resources due to our extractive global economy, which we must change in order to emerge from emergency? Basically, we need an overhaul of our neoliberal economic and financial systems.

The core limiting factor of human well-being is the way in which we have put so much stress on our natural resources and our environment, not to mention the current noticeable change in our societal fabric and communities as a result of COVID-19, including the shift within our cities. There is the reality that more than 50 percent of the urban fabric expected to exist by 2050 has yet to be constructed, and we have not even spoken about inequality. The world's richest 1 percent have more than twice as much wealth as 6.9 billion people, and this is creating a real social tension, which, by the way, is the greatest tipping point and threat to our joint human existence, beyond environmental tipping points. We are facing the threat of climate change and the resulting social tensions that will come with increased conflict, migration, and of course dependencies on scarce resources such as water, food, minerals, and all the bare essentials.

We are our own worst enemy. The human species has forgotten that it is only a fraction of the animal and natural kingdom, and has created a complete imbalance in the natural order of things due to power and profit motives. This is the age where we must shift from "ego" to "eco." What we need to fundamentally understand is the impact of our material footprint on ourselves and the planet. How do we thrive if we do not take into consideration our consumption patterns and the necessary paradigm shift away from an extractive economy? We need to create a fair consumption space that addresses the important role of demand-side management, the real needs of all people, one that takes into consideration the remaining carbon budget and the impact of the wealthiest countries and populations, and that, importantly, ensures a fair and just transition. How do we eliminate overconsumption while enabling everyone to consume enough to be healthy and safe?

That fair consumption space is key. We need to have a guiding framework where we look at overconsumption as the past. Making the future smell good again, as [Hans Joachim] Schellnhuber said before in his opening remarks, is actually understanding our relationship with consumption; coming back to the basics, back to the essentials that we actually learned through COVID-19, that we do not actually need half of the material stuff we have. What is most essential is the way in which we interact with our social system, the fact that our families can thrive and survive when they are hit with systematic and powerful crises.

In fact, our new Earth4All system dynamic modeling has demonstrated what we already knew, that global well-being is declining within our urban areas, but also within our rural communities, which are totally disenfranchised, by the way, from our urban populations and infrastructure. We are seeing a complete disconnect between the wealthiest and the poorest; but also, as wealth has increased for some, the overall well-being of the population has decreased even in wealthy populations.

Therefore, it is time that we shift from wealth for the few to prosperity for the many, and adopt the right criteria and metrics to measure what that actually means, as well as put in place the right guiding principles to ensure success through new governance and leadership models. That is why last year we created the System Change Compass, a compass originally devised to ensure a holistic implementation of the European Green Deal. The Compass is a support tool for President von der Leyen and her Commission, which institutionalizes value-based decision-making through core systems principles and a guiding societal framework for the 21st century. This is important also in terms of the way in which we look at our economic ecosystems, and in particular our industrial ecosystem. We address the need for new economic ecosystems that are value-based and the business models, but also political and investment signals that can drive those shifts. I will not go into each of these individually, but I would like to draw your attention to the potential positive disruption that we now have on our doorstep. This is the moment of truth as short-term value chain disruptions give us the opportunity to transform, and yet in most countries they are currently bringing us back to business as usual rather than advancing the low-carbon and positive social disruption needed. Systemic solutions can address the pressing socioeconomic needs arising from the invasion of Ukraine and accelerate restructuring of the global economy, but we need brave leaders to adopt value-based decision-making and the systems change principles to make this a reality.

This is an important reminder that our unholy dependencies—on certain materials, on certain types of resources, not only fossil energy but industrial agriculture, such as metals and other materials—are being completely shaken to the core, both as a reaction to COVID-19, when we saw disruption throughout the value chains, but also when we look at the disruption now with [the conflict in] Ukraine. Who is feeling the crunch? It is people, because the price of food, materials, and energy is going up. That inequality factor, once again, is fundamental.

We therefore need to look at systemic solutions that can really address these pressing socioeconomic needs, and address the restructuring of the global economy through a 21st-century lens. We must look at the way in which we can address our energy, food, and material dependencies, to come into redundancy, to shift toward service alignment rather than just production alignment, to take into consideration sufficiency and the importance of efficiency.

That is why, building on the tradition of *The Limits to Growth*, the Club of Rome launched in this 50th-anniversary year the Earth4All project with several partners. Earth4All brings together system dynamic modeling with new economic thinking through the 21st Century Transformational Economics Commission. Together, we have assessed how we can actually find the real pathways or turnarounds that are going to enable us to stay within the planetary boundaries. We have come up with five.

[Ending] poverty is absolutely essential. Empowerment of women, in order to ensure access to education, bring women into the formal economy, and into all decision-making structures. Equality, not only between North and South, but within countries. And our relationship with Energy and Food, which are the basic essentials for our survival as we move forward. These are the five global turnarounds that are the most needed: ending poverty, accelerating gender equity, addressing gross inequality, transforming the food system, and transitioning to clean energy. These five turnarounds can truly lead us to greater well-being and prosperity—a well-being for all species and the planet that I would say shifts us away from a consumption model, fully dependent on natural resources use, into a more holistic, balanced model in harmony with nature, and nurturing the garden of the future, which not only smells good but actually makes us survive and thrive in the 21st century.

Within that context, we are looking at new economic models—and we have them! We have the well-being governments that have already put in place well-being economics, and, by the way, have done much better economically through the crisis as they created more resilience in their economies by building in environmental, economic, and social indicators. We also have donut economics and many other new economic models placing social well-being and environmental well-being at the heart of the economy and any political decision-making process.

The Earth4All model as a system dynamic model is continuously taking into consideration the interrelationship between different systems, which is why I love the analogous nonlinear systems thinking that we have referred to across all the different discussions we have had today; the analogy of thriving urban centers and economic communities to anatomic systems, creating systemic anchors in our cities from tree roots to forest canopies all the way to the heavens or to the gods. Everything is interrelated and interdependent.

Understanding and replicating a positive continuum of system dynamics is so important and so urgent if we are to emerge from emergency. We have tried to address this through our analysis of the five turnarounds and the interrelationship between poverty, equality, empowerment, food, and energy, and all the different leverage points that we need in order to truly shift our societal fabric at the global, national, and local levels.

This is the decisive decade. There is no time for complacency, nor despair. We have shifted from Limits to Growth and we now must embrace an Earth for All.

Thank you very much.

⟶

13
toward a circular bioeconomy

Elspeth MacRae

As I listened to [the conference] yesterday and again today, there have been a lot of thoughts, concepts, and commonalities. What I am probably going to show you is that the disruptors are all available right now. They are all there. I am going to give you examples of them as I go through my presentation. I hope you can see how they can all be used for all the things that people have talked about thus far.

If we look at this now-famous planetary boundary picture [Figure 13.1], I wonder, if we drew it again in 2025, *what it might actually look like*. Disruption has been coming for a long time and quite a lot of people have been trying to avoid disruption or prevent disruption, but it is there. Way back in 2013, McKinsey produced a document on it, and since then you can see a huge list of things and there are many more opportunities that have appeared.

I will walk through, in simple language, what bioeconomy is; then circularity; and, finally, evidence and real trustworthy tracking. Tracking is more than just "I have built a house out of wood and I have tracked the wood from the forest and into the house"; it is much more. Then I will briefly mention biomass, because we've got lots of opportunities there—new biomaterials, new manufacturing—and I will finish with urban design.

Fig. 13.1 Planetary boundaries

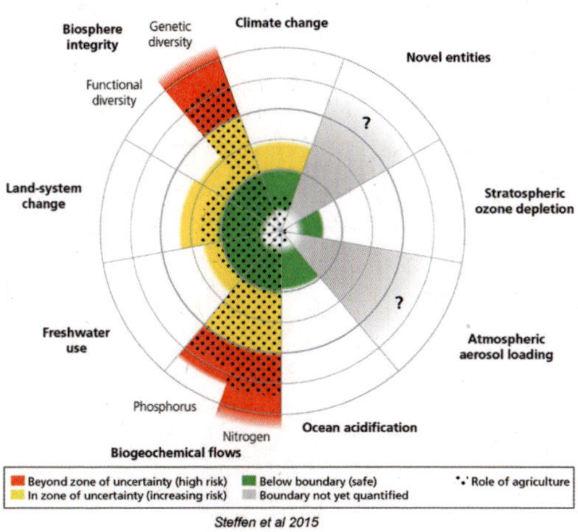

Bioeconomy disrupts centralization: centralized ownership, centralized benefits, centralized manufacturing, and economies of scale. Bioeconomy is a distributed system, with disrupted benefits. You can actually do things with technology these days, which means you do not have to centralize. The scales in bioeconomy tend to be a lot smaller and are additive. Circularity was popularized by the Ellen MacArthur Foundation, and the development of that thinking relies hugely on traceability; performance; many, many cycles; and generations of time. Therefore, you could be thinking 100 or 200 years in the future when you're thinking about circularity and, of course, disruptions to manufacturing.

For example, in New Zealand, there exist cases of bioplastic production. This production begins with trees that capture both CO_2 and water from the atmosphere. They, in turn, through photosynthesis and other processes, convert CO_2 and water into sugars and polymers. These sugars and polymers are taken by microbes that turn them into a storage material just like starch or glycogen for us. This is bioplastic. We take the bioplastic out of those microbes and can make various plastic products. [One example, made in New Zealand,] is bioplastic from polyhydroxyalkanoates (PHAs)[1] made from tree sugars. This can be done with sugars from other waste streams, such as by processing kiwifruit juice; the skins create edible, biodegradable utensils. These bioplastics, because of their PHAs, can be controlled in their degradation because it is a natural process; they regenerate carbon dioxide and water. That is circularity in a nutshell.

Now let us turn to another development of circularity: urban mining. This is Mint Innovation, a New Zealander company that won the Pioneer Award at the World Economic Forum. They mine metals that we throw away. They use microbes to concentrate the metals so that they can be reused. The planet has been doing biology a lot longer than we have been around. Biology is normally nearly 100 percent efficient. Nature does things that we cannot even begin to match artificially. A tree is really just a factory.

In fact, all plants are really just factories; you do not have to think about a tree as solely timber. You can actually think about it more like bamboo, and actually harvest it the same way and use it, replant, and recycle. For example, consider the harvesting of trees, in five rotations, harvested for use in creating biomaterials as an example of future potential (Eisenbies et al. 2014). There is a lot of waste that humans are good at generating, but all of it is usable. Biomaterials can either be used to substitute contemporary materials or be added to contemporary material to render new performance. For example, we can replace asphalt on the roading systems with lignin from trees. In the case of vehicles, if we actually use all the technologies available to us, our vehicles do not need to be full of metal because, if these are autonomously driven and we do not get behind the wheel, no protection is needed, i.e., crashes should no longer occur. An entire vehicle could be made of biobased materials and you can have it generating its own energy from the sun, et cetera. You can absolutely completely reconceive of transport vehicles for people.

Turning now to applications of biomimicry: Figure 13.2 and Figure 13.3 is by designer David Trubridge. These lamps were presented at the Expo2020, Dubai (held from 2021 to 2022). They are made from bioplastic, which I spoke of earlier, and paua shells, a shellfish indigenous to New Zealand that has structural color. The advantage of structural color[2] is that it does not fade. Currently, all the dyes we extract fade, but structural color does not. Paua shell gives you a beautiful structural color that will be there forever. Again, this is an adoption of nature.

Fig. 13.2 Navicula Lamp, by David Trubridge Design[3]

Fig. 13.3 Paua shell provides texture and sparkle, Navicula Lamp (next page)

When we consider new performances with biobased material, we should remember that in the case of engineered woods currently

Fig. 13.4 TERAX pilot plant, Rotorua District Council's Wastewater Treatment Plant

being used to build our tall buildings, these are strips of wood that are glued together for structural strength. That glue could all become biobased, not petroleum based. At present, we do not use the bark from trees that we process for timber, yet bark is full of invaluable materials we can use—for example, suberins,[4] like cork, and tannins,[5] which you can use to make the glues that glue the wood together, and so on and so forth. We can even go as far as using materials from bark for medical applications. Cellulose[6] too is a valuable material from bark that can make many different things. We can even use biomaterials to replace traditional concrete, such as hemp fiber, which can do a better job of insulation (Arehart, Nelson, and Srubar 2020; Arrigoni et al. 2017; Shang and Tariku 2021).

What this all means is that there is already a lot of resistance and rethinking of the industry, and it is distributed (Philp 2018; Bayne et al. 2021; Shapira et al. 2022). I move on to two examples: distributed manufacturing and 4D printing. First, mobile manufacturing: a chemical processing plant; a grass and new compounds processing plant; a mobile pilot plant that processes human waste, making fertilizer and energy [Figure 13.4]; and a cassava waste plant. Instead of gathering waste and transporting it to a factory, mobile plants do the manufacturing locally, keeping wealth within communities.

Finally, 4D printing is an explosion that many people have probably not realized. 3D printing is printing in real time, with less waste.

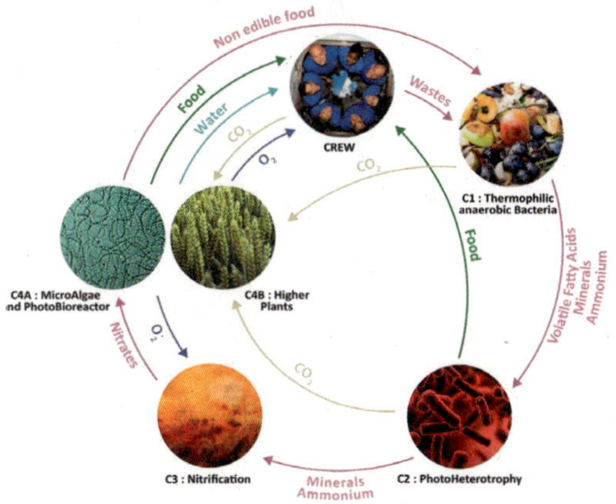

Fig. 13.5 Space station circularity

You can use bio or non-bio materials; in fact, a lot of artificial plastics and metals are used in 3D printing, but they do not have to be. However, in 4D printing, you actually take what biology does and you say, can we get our materials that we have created to do what biology does, that is, respond to environmental cues? An example would be bioplastics that take on one shape when they are wet and another when they are dry. The same can be done with color. Examples include using stem cells and building a living organ for biomedical applications; and extracting lignin from tree waste, electrospinning the lignin into fibers or else combining them with other electrically responsive biomaterials, then using these to help construct actuators for mini robots, ensuring robotic parts are at least partially biobased. There are huge opportunities in this area; just imagine developing 4D printing for housing.

I want to emphasize, because I think people forget about it, the designs we have for living on Mars, and current designs for living on the space station. These are examples of using every biomaterial to the fullest: astronauts have to recycle, recycle, recycle. This should

Fig. 13.6 Mars Ice House section

be inspiring thinking for our own environments on our planet. It is time to use disruption much, much better than we have done.

Fig. 13.7 Mars Ice House yard

I would just say thank you very much for listening. I want to acknowledge some of the people who have done some of the work I have talked about; these are Daniel Gapes, Andrea Stocchero, Rob Lei, NSC SFTI/spearhead 3D/4D printing team, Stefan Hill, Will Barker, Scion, and many other global enthusiasts.

Thank you.

---

1 Polyesters are produced in nature by various microorganisms, as well as through bacterial fermentation of sugars or lipids.

2 Structural color is based on reflection, rather than absorption. These colors are generated by the interaction between incident light and nanostructures.

3 Scion made the material and manufactured the lamp. Designs by David Trubridge Design.

4 A complex polyester, biopolymer is lipophilic, and composed of long-chain fatty acids, called suberin acids, and glycerol.

5 Tannins are a class of astringent, polyphenolic biomolecules that bind to and precipitate proteins and various other organic compounds, including amino acids and alkaloids.

6 A polysaccharide, and the most abundant organic polymer on earth.

References

Arehart, Jay H., William S. Nelson, and Wil V. Srubar III. 2020. "On the Theoretical Carbon Storage and Carbon Sequestration Potential of Hempcrete." *Journal of Cleaner Production* 266: 121846. https://doi.org/10.1016/j.jclepro.2020.121846.

Arrigoni, Alessandro, Renato Pelosato, Paco Melià, Gianluca Ruggieri, Sergio Sabbadini, and Giovanni Dotelli. 2017. "Life Cycle Assessment of Natural Building Materials: The Role of Carbonation, Mixture Components and Transport in the Environmental Impacts of Hempcrete Blocks." *Journal of Cleaner Production* 149: 1051–61. https://doi.org/10.1016/j.jclepro.2017.02.161.

Bayne, Karen, Anita Wreford, Peter Edwards, and Alan Renwick. 2021. "Towards a Bioeconomic Vision for New Zealand: Unlocking Barriers to Enable New Pathways and Trajectories." *New Biotechnology* 60: 138–45. https://doi.org/10.1016/j.nbt.2020.09.004.

Eisenbies, Mark, Timothy Volk, Lawrence Abrahamson, Richard Shuren, Brian Stanton, John Posselius, Matt McArdle, et al. 2014. *Development and Deployment of a Short Rotation Woody Crops Harvesting System Based on a Case New Holland Forage Harvester and SRC Woody Crop Header*. Syracuse: State University of New York College of Environmental Science and Forestry. https://doi.org/10.2172/1164395.

Philp, Jim. 2018. "The Bioeconomy, the Challenge of the Century for Policy Makers." *New Biotechnology* 40, Part A (January 25): 11–19. https://doi.org/10.1016/j.nbt.2017.04.004.

Shang, Yina, and Fitsum Tariku. 2021. "Hempcrete Building Performance in Mild and Cold Climates: Integrated Analysis of Carbon Footprint, Energy, and Indoor Thermal and Moisture Buffering." *Building and Environment* 206: 108377. https://doi.org/10.1016/j.buildenv.2021.108377.

Shapira, Philip, Nicholas E. Matthews, Carrie A. Cizauskas, Emily R. Aurand, Douglas C. Friedman, Donovan S. Layton, Mary E. Maxon, Megan J. Palmer, and Laurence Stamford. 2022. "Building a Bottom-Up Bioeconomy." *Issues in Science and Technology* 38, no. 3 (Spring): 78–83.

Steffen, Will, Katherine Richardson, Johan Rockström, Sarah E. Cornell, Ingo Fetzer, Elena M. Bennett, Reinette Biggs, et al. 2015. "Planetary Boundaries: Guiding Human Development on a Changing Planet." *Science* 347, no. 6223 (January 15). www.science.org/doi/10.1126/science.1259855.

14

paradise found: from mining to gardening

Andrea Gebhard

Dear honorable guests of this important conference, thank you so much for inviting me. I am delighted to be here today. And I would like to show you some of what we are doing in Germany as architects and urban planners.

Has it not always been the dream of humankind to be one with nature? On closer inspection, the interpretation of the creation story is that the beauty of the earth should not be exploited. It is our mandate to take care of the world, to protect it, to cultivate it, and to preserve it. Like a good shepherd, humankind should be responsible for the creation, the fertilization, and the care of the earth, not the subjection of nature. As Pope Francis has said, the climate is a common good for everyone. It belongs to all and is meant for all. On a global level, the complex climate system is linked to many of the essential conditions for human life.

However, we have been aware of the inconvenient truth for a long time. Since *Limits to Growth*, we know that our view of the landscape as pure capital, whose resources can be freely exploited, has reached its limit and threatens our very existence on earth.

Emissions from the construction sector are projected at 38 percent, but in truth, some emissions from transport also fall in this category. This brings us to 40 percent projected emissions for the segment built environment (UNEP 2020). It is not right. Yet this is how we build. I have listened to the impressive knowledge and experience in this room, yet we still haven't succeeded in implementing the drastic changes the planet needs. How can we change? We only have 16 years to go on the way we currently do. Time is pressing and we have to create new systems. We have to put a new lens on all this. Traditional methods of mastering nature are behind us; we should reconsider the primacy of technical solutions.

We described all our efforts in yesterday's and today's presentation. And now what can we do? Perhaps a holistic approach is better. A holistic approach through landscape. Friedrich Franz von Anhalt-Dessau recommended looking at the world as a garden. In a garden, you see the environment, you see the trees and the plants, they are

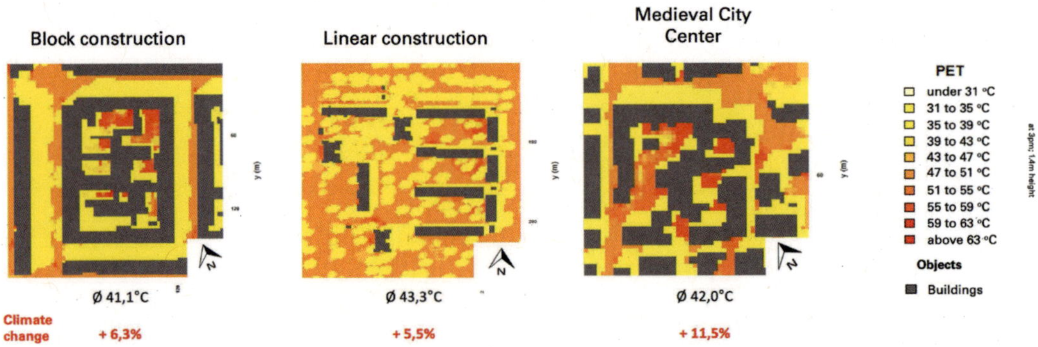

Fig. 14.1 Thermal load on a hot day, Munich grid simulation

beautiful and they smell good. They evoke joy every day and you will take care of it. You take care of it as a routine. You will not destroy it.

As architects, interior architects, landscape architects, and urban planners, we are partly responsible for the global problems, but also part of the solution. We can change the world when we prioritize the environmental challenges: the burning tundras, the floods. Take any industrial area near Munich: no green roofs, and no facade greening. But we could easily do it, right? Plus, we could use solar panels. Also, we increasingly live in individualized property, but we should be thriving in the commons. We need to change our buildings and we need to change the way we live.

In every planning assignment, we need to look at what we are planning and where we are planning it. In my opinion, the best thing is to have a deep understanding of the climate of the planning site as a specific area or neighborhood. For example, when you look at the climate of Munich, you can see heating effects of different urban patterns. With the effects of climate change, we know that block patterns will raise city temperatures by 6 percent. Linear city patterns will raise city temperatures by 5 percent, and medieval city forms will raise city temperatures by 11 percent. However, if we create green infrastructures with trees, we can lower city temperatures by 13 percent. Green roofs lower urban temperatures by 5 percent, and green facades by 10 percent (Centre for Urban Ecology and Climate Adaptation 2020, 40).

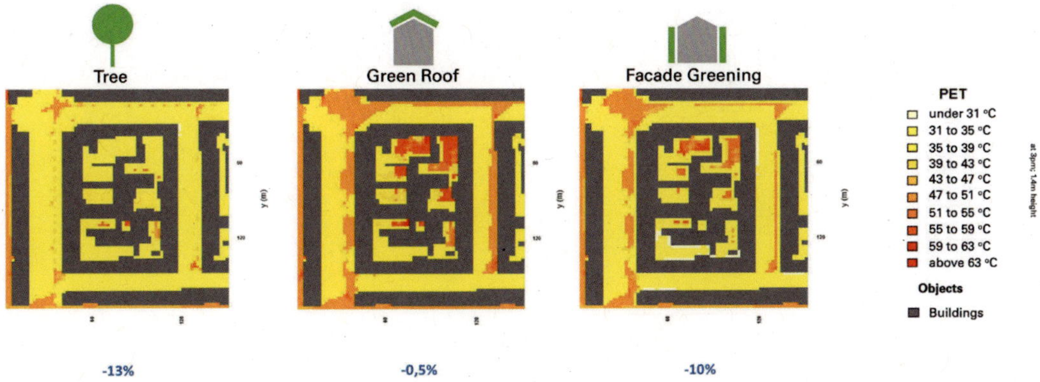

Fig. 14.2 Effect of green infrastructure, Munich grid simulation

Perhaps gardening the city is indeed a better way for building. The idea is not new. We do not have to build everything new; we can use the things we already have. I call this golden energy instead of gray energy. We have to build in a value-preserving way, with wood, combined with concrete. And open spaces are the key, the basis for all planning intentions. How can we get there? How many open spaces do we have in a city? How can we help people to stay in a city center, to have a good life in the city? We have all these green spaces in the city. Our office was invited for studies for Munich and Regensburg, and after we talked to the municipality, our suggestion for well-balanced green city spaces was: four square meters per person at a distance of 250 meters or a five-minute walking distance to six square meters per person at a distance of 500 meters or a 10-minute walking distance.

Usually, you have grids all over the city. In this grid from Munich (see Figures 14.1 and 14.2), you can see the cooling that will help us to make the city livable, with a healthy environment and high quality of life. Figures 14.1 and 14.2 are a re-creation of what cooling means: with evaporation and transpiration from trees, cooling improves. In the future, a strong city will be one that preserves water and uses it for everything.

The natural resources and the landscape must be the basis of all spatial planning and our design. The postulated *Bauwende*, with all its dependencies and effects, takes place in urban and rural spaces. Therefore, the cooperation between architecture, urban planning, landscape planning, engineering sciences, and agricultural planning must be repositioned and implemented in a transdisciplinary manner. For this purpose, the institutional and technical fragmentation of the disciplines must be overcome, a transdisciplinary culture must be developed, and urban, mobility, and landscape planning must be consistently integrated.

A roof is approximately a fifth of a facade. We should urgently build roofs in better ways. Also, the facades can be one of the best things for biodiversity in cities. It is less expensive. The operation cost of a green facade is €1,300 a year, and the operation cost for a normal facade is €16,525 a year. [Elspeth MacRae] spoke about urban farming. It is one of the most important things we have to do. Let me turn to wetlands. Energy or food production goes hand in hand with the use of the country. Wetlands must stay wet. Currently, these areas continuously leak about 1.9 gigatons of CO_2 per year from the cultivation of corn or other agricultural production (Umweltbundesamt 2022). This is too dangerous for us. We know that the wetlands can absorb 700 tons of carbon per hectare per year. That is six times more than in forests (LUBW, n.d.). What can we do, and how can we do it?

If we state that species extinction, CO_2 emissions, water pollution, water shortage, and soil erosion are originally caused by the material cycle between city and country, and agricultural production has a significant impact on the earth's resources, it becomes clear that the agricultural production must also take place in the city, in the immediate vicinity of consumers.

Only if we manage to face the fundamental questions with a holistic approach in spatial planning can we approach the planning goal of preserving the world for all species. That means we have to define goals, develop plans, and get people excited about them. It is up to us to redefine and implement a future-proof, resilient development for cities and countryside.

Let me come to an end by telling you what I think we should do. These are the legal building regulations the city of Munich has introduced: ... If you want to get permission to build, you have to have a green design at the planning stage. You have to design the pathways and driveways. You have to implement green roofs. Without a green roof, you cannot get a building permit. Without the combination of greening and photovoltaics, you will not get permission. If you do not have a green facade, you will not get permission. Also, for an underground garage, you have to do new things. Also for parking areas and for rainwater management. We should come together and say, we know everything, we know how we can deal with it. Let us make them law. I have been in my profession for 35 years and I was always fighting for such things to have regulations.

Finally, we have to talk about sustainability and put ecology first. If you do not put ecology first, this planet will not be fit for us to live on. The planet will survive without us. Since we are in the Vatican, I also have a suggestion that for every Catholic in the world, Pope Francis and [Cardinal Turkson] plant one tree in the next two years.

Thank you very much.

References

Centre for Urban Ecology and Climate Adaptation. 2020. *Guidelines for Climate-Oriented Communities in Bavaria*. Munich: Technical University of Munich. www.zsk.tum.de/fileadmin/w00bqp/www/PDFs/Guideline_English_final-komprimiert.pdf.

LUBW (Landesanstalt für Umwelt Baden-Württemberg). n.d. "Moorböden." Accessed January 29, 2023. www.lubw.baden-wuerttemberg.de/klimawandel-und-anpassung/moorboeden.

Umweltbundesamt. 2022. "Emissionen der Landnutzung, -änderung und Forstwirtschaft." *Umweltbundesamt.de*, March 21, 2022. www.umweltbundesamt.de/daten/klima/treibhausgas-emissionen-in-deutschland/emissionen-der-landnutzung-aenderung#bedeutung-von-landnutzung-und-forstwirtschaft.

UNEP (United Nations Environment Programme). 2020. *2020 Global Status Report for Buildings and Construction: Towards a Zero-Emission, Efficient and Resilient Buildings and Construction Sector*. Nairobi, Kenya: UN Environment Programme.

15
sustainable forest manage-ment

Marc Palahí, Fredric Mosley, and Venla Wallius

Thank you to the Pontifical Academy of Sciences for inviting me[1] here today. It is a pleasure. It has been inspiring to see that all the speakers yesterday and today have mentioned forest, trees, or wood. As a forest scientist, this is encouraging. Today, I would like to share a few reflections and facts on the important transformational role of our forests, sustainable forest management, and forest-based solutions in rethinking our economy and the Anthropocene or the Urbanocene, as Dr. [Geoffrey] West mentioned yesterday.

Let us start at the very beginning. Before trees and forests emerged on our planet, our planet was 8°C warmer than it is now, and had eight times the CO_2 levels it does today (Stanley and Luczaj 1999). But with the emergence of trees and the expansion of forests, the climate of earth radically changed. This happened because trees use solar energy to transform water and CO_2 into biochemical energy, while at the same time releasing oxygen and water in vapor format. Therefore, with the expansion of forests, a planetary cooling effect took place. No wonder that the tree of life is an important archetype in many cultures and religions across the world. In fact, trees and forests support life beyond their own boundaries because, in addition to hosting biodiversity, they are key for the water and carbon cycle on earth. Forests transformed the planet once, and now we need them to transform our world so that the planet continues to be habitable for future generations. This is crucial, because after relying for 150 years on a linear fossil economy, we have arrived at a tipping point.

In fact, the multidimensional crises that we are facing today in terms of climate, biodiversity, inequality, and health are not different crises. They are just different consequences of the same fundamental problem: our economic system. It is a system addicted to fossil resources, but also to growth at all costs; an economic system that fails to value our most important capital, and the basis for human health and well-being: nature. Having arrived at such a tipping point, we should remember the words of Albert Einstein, who used to say that "we cannot solve our current problems with the same thinking we used when we created them." This is exactly the way of thinking we need now in order to create a new economic paradigm. To do that,

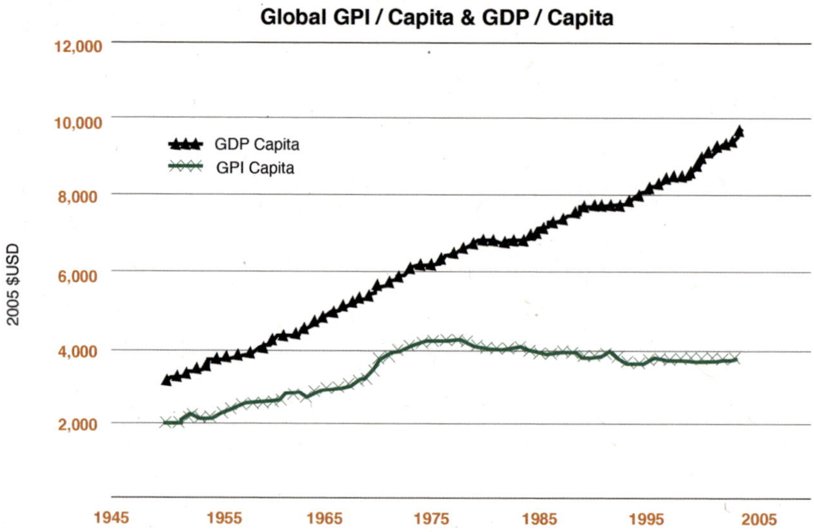

Fig. 15.1 Global GPI/capita and GDP/capita

we need to start by valuing and measuring economic progress in a different way.

Nowadays, Gross Domestic/National Product (GDP/GNP) is used as a standard measure of economic welfare. However, in 1934, Simon Kuznets, the economist who developed the concept, told the US Congress not to focus narrowly on GNP/GDP because it is not a measure of welfare or progress. In 1968, Robert F. Kennedy said that [GNP] measures everything except what matters in life. Additionally, the problem with GNP/GDP is that the measure has become the target, and when a measure becomes the target, it is no longer a good measure. Figure 15.1 shows a comparison of GDP and a Genuine Progress Indicator[2] (GPI) over the last few decades. It shows that if we measure economic progress according to GPI, the world has been in recession since the 1970s.

Having said that, now let's reflect about the role cities will need to play in transforming our world to ensure a sustainable future. Cities, which are our main economic and innovation hubs, but also our main consumers of resources, energy, and food, have a responsibility to lead the transition from the current linear and fossil economy to a circular bioeconomy. Remember that *bio* means life. A circular bioeconomy is, above all, an economy where life, not consumption, becomes its true engine and purpose. A circular bioeconomy, for me, is an economy that prospers in harmony with nature, but it is also powered by nature. This is not a contradiction; it is a necessary condition because, at the end of the day, we need to restore harmony between humanity and nature.

Circular bioeconomy is basically an economy that uses renewable energy and manages, sustainably, our biological systems in a holistic manner to produce, in a synergistic way, food, energy, ecosystem services, and biobased solutions to decarbonize our economy. It is also fundamental to recognize that the circular bioeconomy is ultimately powered by biodiversity, because biodiversity ensures that life is capable of adapting and evolving in a changing environment. As you mentioned before, John [Schellnhuber], our linear fossil economy has been obsessed with efficiency, yet in nature and complex systems, everything is about resilience and adaptability. Therefore, a circular bioeconomy should place biodiversity at the center. It is also important to recognize that a circular bioeconomy is much more complex than a fossil economy, because living systems are complex by nature. This means that for the circular bioeconomy to succeed, it needs to be knowledge intensive, which means looking beyond natural sciences for transdisciplinary collaboration.

We need to draw on Indigenous knowledge and ancestral knowledge, which is abundant. It should also be innovation driven, because we need to really think outside the box in the current context. The complexity of a circular bioeconomy brings many possibilities, because if we look at how biological resources are owned, distributed, managed, and processed compared with fossil resources, they offer opportunities for distributing jobs and infrastructures. If we do the governance right, the circular bioeconomy, as [Elspeth MacRae] mentioned, provides us with an opportunity to address inequality. Finally, it is not only about knowledge and science, but about translating that into wisdom. This is why we need to use circular economy principles: reuse, recycle, repair, and reduce consumption. These are four important principles when talking about a circular bioeconomy and also when we talk about a sustainable forest economy.

Let me move on to forests. We have heard a lot of discussions about forests and trees over the past few days. Forests are central for transitioning from a linear fossil economy toward a circular bioeconomy. Why? They are the most important biological infrastructure on the planet. This is not only because they cover 31 percent of the land, equivalent to 4 billion hectares (FAO and UNEP 2020), but because forests are the cities of nature, and trees are the buildings. Forests host 80 percent of the terrestrial biological diversity (FAO 2020) and are our largest terrestrial carbon sink (Pan et al. 2011). They are also a major terrestrial source for precipitation and oxygen.

Due to the planetary role of forests in the water cycle, they are also crucial for food security, and in that sense they have transcontinental implications. Figure 15.2 shows the distribution of the world's forests.

Out of the 4 billion hectares of forests that we have on the planet, 34 percent can be categorized as primary forest (FAO 2020). In the West, we often think of primary forests as being untouched, but this is not so, as Anna María [Durán Calisto] demonstrated in her presentation yesterday. Often, these areas are inhabited by Indigenous

Fig. 15.2 The global distribution of forests

The global distribution of forests, by climatic domain

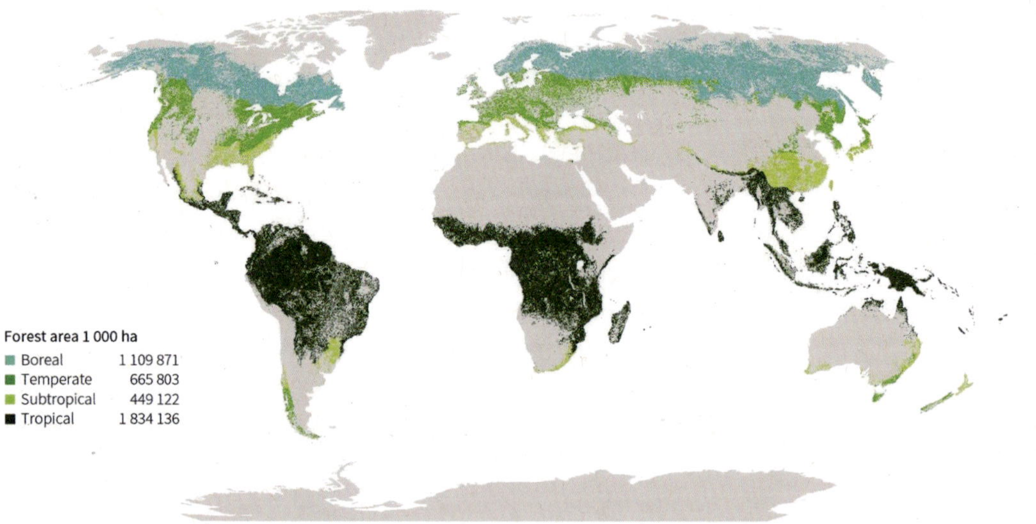

Source: Adapted from United Nations World map, 2020.

FAO. 2020. *Global Forest Resources Assessment 2020.* Rome.

people, and under their stewardship the forests have been utilized for thousands of years in a sustainable way, following ecological principles.

Another category is intensively managed even-aged forest plantations, which make up 3 percent of the world's forests (FAO and UNEP 2020). They provide approximately 35 percent of round wood in the world (Jürgensen, Kollert, and Lebedys 2014). The rest of the world's forests, 63 percent, are so-called seminatural forests, and they are managed under different types of intensity.

Let me summarize a few challenges and opportunities for sustainable forest management at the global level. First of all, deforestation is still a huge problem. We are still losing an average of 10 million hectares every year (FAO and UNEP 2020). Remember, nearly 90 percent of global deforestation is driven by agriculture: 50 percent is for cropland expansion, and 38 percent is related to livestock grazing (FAO 2022). Unless we address the food challenge, we will not address the deforestation problem. By preventing deforestation, we would avoid 6.7 billion tons of CO_2 emissions every year (Friedlingstein et al. 2022). This would have a substantial impact on the climate. As I mentioned before, a key challenge is to protect the primary forests. In that context, respecting the rights of Indigenous communities is crucial.

Regarding restoration, the previous speakers have addressed this topic perfectly. Just to mention here, as Tony [Rinaudo] mentioned, the restoration-reforestation challenge is not so much about trees as it is about people. Many reforestation programs in the world have failed because they believe that planting the tree is the end of the project, but it is just the beginning. If we do not empower local communities and they do not see the economic, social, and environmental benefits, it will not work. You need to provide the necessary tools and knowledge to local communities so that they will be the ones that benefit and immediately connect restoration-reforestation with value chains.

Within sustainable forest management and adaptation, we increasingly see that many of our forests are at a tipping point, which is worrying. The impacts of climate change and natural disturbances are destroying many of our forests. For example, for the last 20 years, Canada's forests have been emitting CO_2 rather than sequestering it, due to factors such as forest fires and the impacts of bark beetles (Environment and Climate Change Canada 2022). The problem with the impacts of climate change on our forests is not what we already know, but what we do not know because of the nonlinearity of our systems. In order to prepare for these future threats, more investments in climate-smart forestry and adaptation strategies are required.

Fig. 15.3 Marc and José in Sharamentsa, Ecuador

Finally, the good news is that with the new science and technology of the last few years, we can transform wood resources into a totally new range of biobased solutions. Our colleagues from New Zealand, [Dr. Amanda Yates and Elspeth MacRae], already mentioned many different alternatives. I will touch on two important ones. The obvious one is the potential of wood in decarbonizing the building and construction sector. This has been addressed here by numerous speakers. You have already seen, during the last two days, that wood is the only significant construction material, together with bamboo, that can be grown sustainably. Using wood is important because you avoid a great amount of carbon emissions compared with the use of concrete and steel (Leskinen et al. 2018). In addition, for every cubic meter of engineered wood products that you use, you store around a ton of CO_2 (European Committee for Standardization 2014; Churkina et al. 2020). In this way, you can transform buildings and cities into carbon storage infrastructures.

I wanted to say a few words about the fashion industry, because President von der Leyen mentioned that the fashion industry is also one of the main offenders in our economy, responsible for approximately 8 to 10 percent of the global carbon emissions (Niinimäki et al. 2020) and 35 percent of oceanic microplastic pollution (Boucher and Friot 2017, 43). This is largely due to polyester and other synthetic fibers, which make up 65 percent of our textiles (Textile Exchange 2022).

Cotton is also not sustainable because it uses a lot of pesticides and fertilizers (Muthu et al. 2012; Shen, Worrell, and Patel 2010). Wood would be a solution. We now have the technology to transform wood into sustainable textiles with a significantly smaller carbon footprint than polyester or cotton (Felgueiras et al. 2021; Shen, Worrell, and Patel 2010). Again, the problem of fashion is not only the type of raw material but the fact that consumption is accelerating. An average person now uses around 60 percent more clothes than at the beginning of the century, but they're wearing them only half as long (Remy, Speelman, and Swartz 2016).

To conclude, I wanted to mention that this year I had the chance to spend several days living in the middle of the Amazon forests with the Achuar Indigenous communities in Ecuador [Figure 15.3]. It was inspiring, because there I saw two worlds colliding. There was a dying world, powered by an extractive fossil economy. Then I saw a totally different world, the Indigenous world, a living world, full of respect for nature. The Indigenous peoples do not only have great knowledge on nature, forests, plants, and animals, but what impressed me was their capacity to translate that knowledge into wisdom.

This is what's missing in Western societies. The West is effective in translating science into technology to solve problems that we create for ourselves. Here, with the Achuar, I learned that they are wise enough not to create problems, wise enough to live in harmony with nature.

1 Marc Palahí was the speaker at the conference.

2 GDP adjusted for social and natural capital.

References

Boucher, Julien, and Damien Friot. 2017. *Primary Microplastics in the Oceans: A Global Evaluation of Sources*. Gland, Switzerland: IUCN.

Churkina, Galina, Alan Organschi, Christopher P.O. Reyer, Andrew Ruff, Kira Vinke, Zhu Liu, Barbara K. Reck, T.E. Graedel, and Hans Joachim Schellnhuber. 2020. "Buildings as a Global Carbon Sink." *Nature Sustainability* 3, no. 4: 269–76. http://doi: 10.1038/s41893-019-0462-4.

Environment and Climate Change Canada. 2022. *National Inventory Report 1990–2020: Greenhouse Gas Sources and Sinks in Canada: Canada's Submission to the United Nations Framework Convention on Climate Change*. Gatineau, Canada:

Environment and Climate Change Canada. https://publications.gc.ca/collections/collection_2022/eccc/En81-4-2020-1-eng.pdf.

European Committee for Standardization. 2014. *CSN EN 16449: Wood and Wood-Based Products: Calculation of the Biogenic Carbon Content of Wood and Conversion to Carbon Dioxide*. Brussels: CEN.

FAO. 2020. *Global Forest Resources Assessment 2020: Main Report*. Rome: Food and Agriculture Organization of the United Nations. https://doi.org/10.4060/ca9825en.

———. 2022. *FRA 2020 Remote Sensing Survey*. FAO Forestry Paper no. 186. Rome: Food and Agriculture Organization of the United Nations. https://doi.org/10.4060/cb9970en.

FAO and UNEP. 2020. *The State of the World's Forests 2020: Forests, Biodiversity and People*. Rome: Food and Agriculture Organization of the United Nations and UN Environment Programme. https://doi.org/10.4060/ca8642en.

Felgueiras, Catarina, Nuno G. Azoia, Cidália Gonçalves, Miguel Gama, and Fernando Dourado. 2021. "Trends on the Cellulose-Based Textiles: Raw Materials and Technologies." *Frontiers in Bioengineering and Biotechnology* 9 (March 29). https://doi.org/10.3389/fbioe.2021.608826.

Friedlingstein, Pierre, Michael O'Sullivan, Matthew W. Jones, Robbie M. Andrew, Luke Gregor, Judith Hauck, Corinne le Quéré, et al. 2022. "Global Carbon Budget 2022." *Earth System Science Data* 14, no. 11: 4811–4900. https://doi.org/10.5194/essd-14-4811-2022.

Jürgensen, C., W. Kollert, and A. Lebedys. 2014. *Assessment of Industrial Roundwood Production from Planted Forests*. Planted Forests and Trees Working Paper 48. Rome: Food and Agriculture Organization of the United Nations. www.fao.org/3/i3384e/i3384e.pdf.

Kubiszewski, Ida, Robert Costanza, Carol Franco, Philip Lawn, John Talberth, Tim Jackson, and Camille Aylmer. 2013. "Beyond GDP: Measuring and Achieving Global Genuine Progress." *Ecological Economics* 93 (September): 57–68. https://doi.org/10.1016/j.ecolecon.2013.04.019.

Leskinen, Pekka, Giuseppe Cardellini, Sara González-García, Elias Hurmekoski, Roger Sathre, Jyri Seppälä, Carolyn Smyth, Tobias Stern, and Pieter Johannes Verkerk. 2018. *Substitution Effects of Wood-Based Products in Climate Change Mitigation*. From Science to Policy 7. Joensuu, Finland: European Forest Institute. https://doi.org/10.36333/fs07.

Muthu, Subramanian Senthilkannan, Y. Li, J.Y. Hu, and P.Y. Mok. 2012. "Quantification of Environmental Impact and Ecological Sustainability for Textile Fibres." *Ecological Indicators* 13, no. 1: 66–74. https://doi.org/10.1016/j.ecolind.2011.05.008.

Niinimäki, Kirsi, Greg Peters, Helena Dahlbo, Patsy Perry, Timo Rissanen, and Alison Gwilt. 2020. "The Environmental Price of Fast Fashion." *Nature Reviews: Earth and Environment* 1: 189–200. https://doi.org/10.1038/s43017-020-0039-9.

Pan, Yude, Richard A. Birdsey, Jingyun Fang, Richard Houghton, Pekka E. Kauppi, Werner A. Kurz, Oliver L. Phillips, et al. 2011. "A Large and Persistent Carbon Sink in the World's Forests." *Science* 333, no. 6045: 988–93. https://doi.org/10.1126/science.1201609.

Remy, Nathalie, Eveline Speelman, and Steven Swartz. 2016. "Style That's Sustainable: A New Fast-Fashion Formula." *McKinsey Sustainability*, October 20, 2016.

Shen, Li, Ernst Worrell, and Martin K. Patel. 2010. "Environmental Impact Assessment of Man-Made Cellulose Fibers." *Resources, Conservation and Recycling* 55, no. 2 (December): 260–74. https://doi.org/10.1016/j.resconrec.2010.10.001.

Stanley, Steven M., and John A. Luczaj. 1999. *Earth System History*. New York: W.H. Freeman.

Textile Exchange. 2022. *Preferred Fiber & Materials: Market Report 2021*. https://textileexchange.org/wp-content/uploads/2022/10/Textile-Exchange_PFMR_2022.pdf.

16
utopia or oblivion

Carlo Ratti

Good morning, everyone. I was asked to talk about the relationship between design and digitization in the context of the New European Bauhaus. My presentation is titled "Utopia or Oblivion," which is an expression that comes from Richard Buckminster Fuller (1970), the great American architect and inventor of the mid-twentieth century. Fuller first used these words in the 1960s, when the world was obviously quite different from today. But his underlying message is still valid, perhaps even more so. Today we find ourselves at a historical crossroads. We are facing an unprecedented climate crisis. As citizens and designers, we must decide where we want to focus our attention. And the choice, once again, is between Utopia or Oblivion.

Now let me be clear. If we keep thinking that the purpose of design is beautifying existing objects, then it is going to be Oblivion. In this slide[1] you see a stunning collection of chairs. Each of them is certainly a beautiful product. But the point is, we already have billions of chairs on our planet. As designers, planners, and architects, should we focus our efforts on designing and producing more and more objects or on helping to fight climate change?

The only way for designers to pursue the road to Utopia is by tackling our collective challenges, and by making this higher aim the first priority of our work. Of course, that is not easy. It requires a change in mindset as well as a change in methodology. But there is a place where we can start. It's the city.

Now, consider these four numbers: 2, 55, 75, and 80 (Ratti 2021). Cities are only 2 percent of the surface of the earth, but they house 55 percent of the human population, and they are responsible for 75 percent of global energy consumption and for 80 percent of total CO_2 emissions. In other words, if we can do something—even something relatively small—to make our cities a bit more sustainable, that can generate a significant ripple effect globally.

What kind of tools can we use to achieve this objective? I would argue that the most interesting potential comes from integrating digital technologies into the built environment. In the last two decades, we have witnessed the emergence of a new technological paradigm.

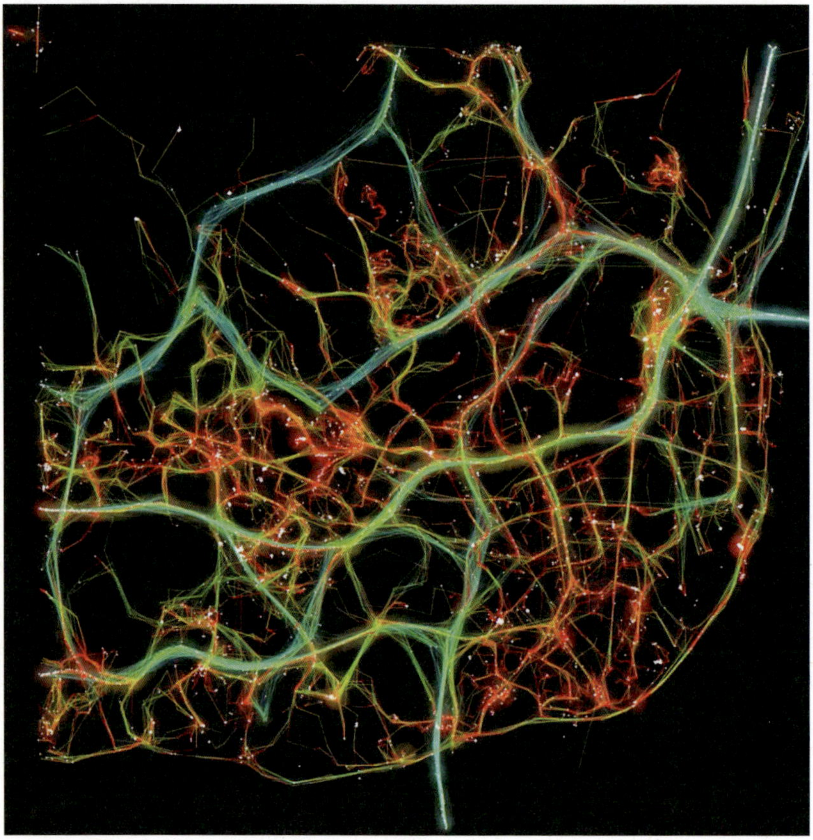

Fig. 16.1 Lisbon traffic visualization by Pedro M. Cruz

We have observed the internet entering into physical space, becoming the so-called Internet of Things. This kind of transformation is having a profound impact in many spheres of our daily life. When every single object becomes connected, we get an unprecedented amount of data that tells us how people move and behave in the city. This data is already reshaping the way we understand the built environment, and if used in a smart way, it can lead to a more sustainable urban life.

As a first step, digital technologies can be a medium to observe the city as we have never seen it before. For instance, Figure 16.1 shows a visualization of Lisbon [traffic] made by Pedro M. Cruz, a former researcher at our Senseable City Lab at MIT. This visualization was developed using billions of data points collected from the local taxi network. The data gives us opportunities for in-depth analysis, and results that can guide us toward more informed perspectives and better design. In this animation, we can see that the city looks almost like a living organism.

To give you a more concrete example of how digital and physical elements interact with one another, I want to tell you about a project our design practice CRA-Carlo Ratti Associati is currently developing. It is called Helsinki Hot Heart (CRA 2021) and is a complex work of urban infrastructure that would not be possible without data and artificial intelligence.

Hot Heart was the result of a competition launched by the city of Helsinki called the Helsinki Energy Challenge (City of Helsinki, n.d.). It was a rather extraordinary competition, conceived with the objective of gathering ideas for decarbonizing the city's district heating by 2030. Currently, the district heating system in Helsinki relies on power plants, which simultaneously produce electricity and hot water for powering and heating the city. However, these plants are run on coal, and are a major source of Helsinki's carbon footprint.

The municipality has decided to discontinue these power plants in a few years. Therefore, the real question was: What technologies can we use to help decarbonize the local district heating? What made this competition stand out is that, usually, municipal governments follow established best practices in determining urban policies. However, the magnitude of the climate crisis we are facing is so great that our past case studies cannot offer an adequate solution for it. Sometimes, when you want to speed up innovation, you need to take a totally different road. With its Energy Challenge, the city of Helsinki did precisely that. It went against the grain and called for "moonshot" thinking.[2]

The competition attracted over 250 applications from all over the world, including some of the world's major companies and agencies. From these proposals, the city of Helsinki selected 10 finalists, and announced the winners in early 2021. Our design practice led one of the winning teams, and since then we have been working with the municipality to implement the solution.

This experience gave us several insights into how to foster forward-thinking urban ideas. First of all, interdisciplinary collaboration is crucial. Our designers based in New York led the project, working together with engineering firms such as Ramboll, Transsolar, SBP, and multinational companies like Danfoss or Schneider Electric. OP Financial Group helped us with financials, while the British media agency Squint/Opera has been helping in communicating the project to a broader public.

Second, we leveraged the power of data to address today's key issue in decarbonization. If we look at the costs of renewable energy production, and wind power prices in particular, we can see that they have fallen quite significantly. Today, all around the planet, you can produce a megawatt hour of renewable energy for between $20 and $30. This is all good news. But there is still one critical problem with renewable energy sources: their intermittency. Sometimes you could use too much while producing too little.

One megawatt hour can be produced at a cost of between $20 and $30, whether the power comes from the sun or wind. However, if you need to store $20 or $30 worth of energy today, it requires over $200,000, which is what you see to the left of Figure 16.2. While looking at this gigantic cost gap, we came up with an idea: Instead of power, can we store heat? It turns out that if we create an infrastructure that works like a thermal battery, the cost per megawatt hour will no longer be $200,000, but closer to $200 per megawatt hour. To make this battery, we propose transferring hot water into giant containers, floating in the ocean, that retain their heat for hours thanks to the high heat capacity of H_2O. When the wind stops blowing and the sun stops shining, the hot water can be pumped into homes.

However, if you want to do this, you need to have a lot of control. You need a smart grid, and artificial intelligence to manage all the pieces. This includes the different sources of heat and energy—the solar panels and the wind turbines—the gigantic thermal batteries that store their output, and the systems that transfer the reserved heat into the city itself.

Our design for the Helsinki Hot Heart allows many different types of energy to power the system, because we do not know exactly what mix will be available to us. Wind is clearly the best energy source in Finland and other Nordic countries, but that mix might change with the development of new technologies, so you want the system to adapt to different future scenarios.

There are additional benefits. Not only can the Hot Heart synchronize demand and supply behind the whole power grid, but the giant floating structures can also become public spaces. This seemingly trivial benefit is actually vital, because it gives the project a built-in way to engage with citizens, teach them something visible and legible, and give them a stake in the struggle against climate change.

How can we turn the Hot Heart into a heart for people? We will cover the top of our floating heat-storing batteries with domes and populate the newfound space with forests. Figure 16.3 shows the exterior. Inside these biodomes, we plan to create an ecosystem

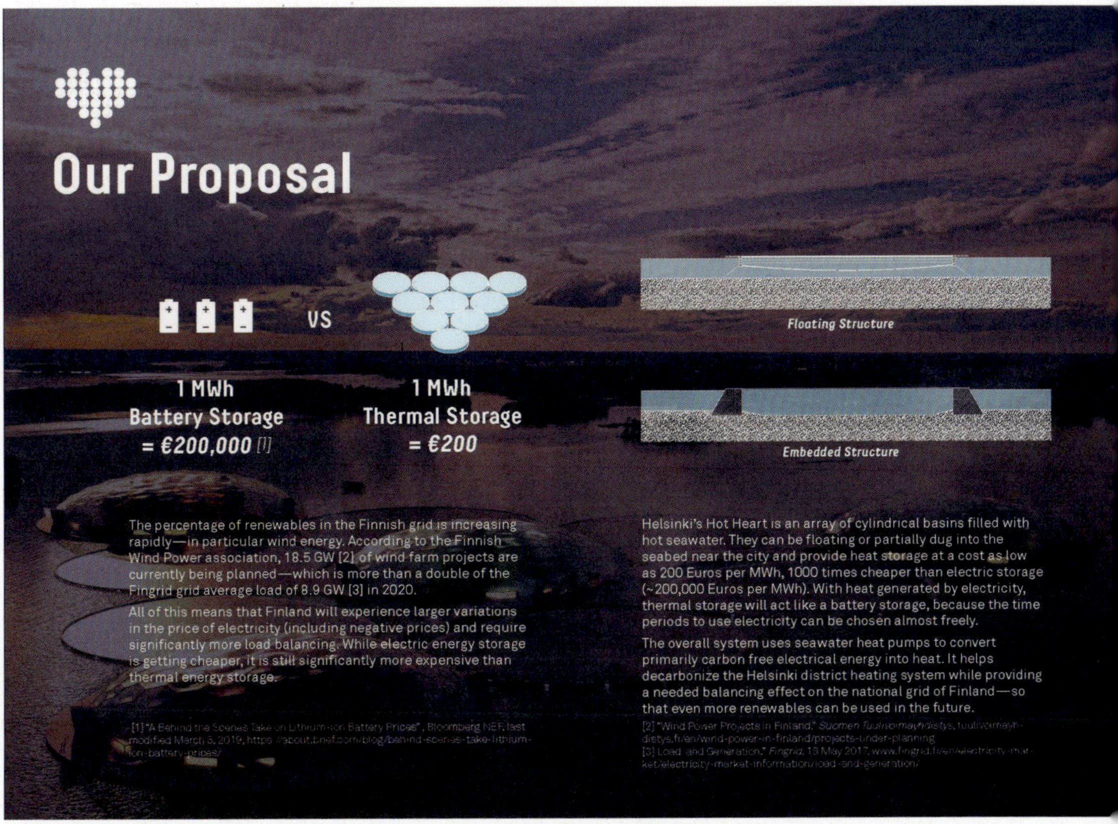

Fig. 16.2 Proposal for Helsinki's Hot Heart

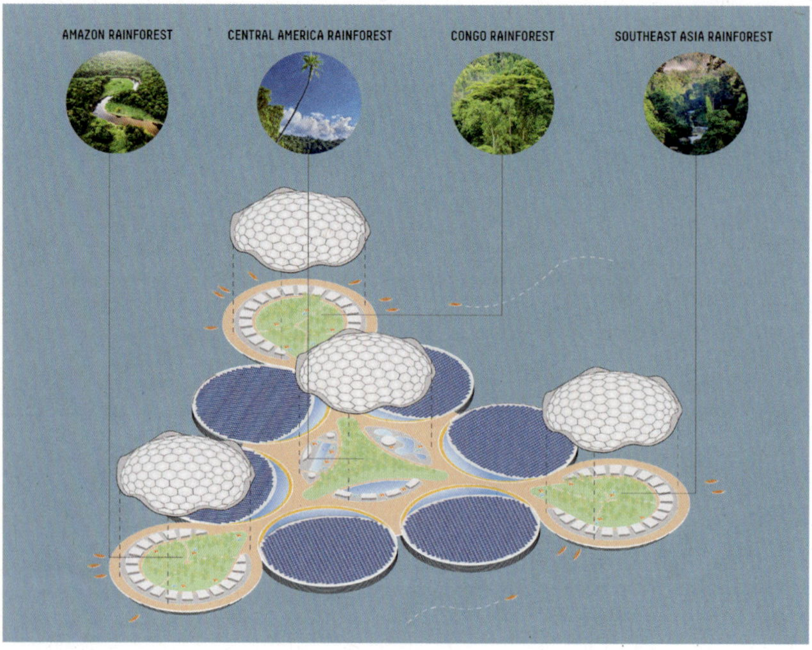

Fig. 16.3 Biodome ecosystems render for Helsinki's Hot Heart proposal

blending elements of four tropical forests around the planet: in Central America, South America, Africa, and Asia. Citizens will be welcome to relax and socialize in the green space inside, and experience firsthand that sustainability is not only about austerity.

This project will help Helsinki meet its decarbonization goals by the end of the decade, storing all the heat it needs in any given year—around 6,000 gigawatt hours. From a financial point of view, the investment could have good returns. Since the thermal energy is generated when the production costs are minimal, it brings down the prices of using that energy throughout the day. Based on our calculations, people could pay 10 percent less than they do now to consume the same amount of energy.

Looking beyond Helsinki, Hot Heart could work just as well in cities with extreme climates that require either heating or cooling for extended periods during the year. It allows the grid to be powered by renewable energy while overcoming the challenges of intermittency we now face.

This example is a gateway for us to arrive at the understanding that the digital is changing the way we understand cities. Most interestingly, when data and artificial intelligence are incorporated into infrastructure and the urban fabric, we can really change the paradigm in terms of thinking about where we live, and make Fuller's utopian scenario a reality. Thank you.

---

1 Carlo Ratti is referring to The Chair Collection Poster, Vitra Design Museum, 2022, composed of 224 iconic chair designs.

2 *Moonshot* is a word used in the field of innovation to describe the approach of choosing a huge, seemingly insurmountable problem and proposing a radical solution. The idea is not to look for small, incremental improvements, but to aim for a huge improvement or solution.

References

City of Helsinki. n.d. *Helsinki Energy Challenge*. Accessed January 31, 2023. https://energychallenge.hel.fi/.

CRA-Carlo Ratti Associati. 2021. *The Hot Heart of Helsinki*. https://thehotheart.com.

Fuller, R. Buckminster. 1970. *Utopia or Oblivion: The Prospects for Humanity*. London: Allen Lane.

Ratti, Carlo. 2021. "La Sfida Parte Dalle Città: Il Cuore Caldo di Helsinki." Edited by Marta Dassù. *Aspenia* 93 (June): 106–9.

→

17
roof over our heads: examining adaptation for those living informally

Sheela Patel

Climate change and the challenges of balancing climate justice with reduction of carbon emissions requires attention to how, both locally and globally, the challenges faced by vulnerable communities, households, and individuals is addressed in this context, not only on behalf of the urban poor but on behalf of a range of people, many of whom have lived in informal settlements for three generations, especially in the Global South.

Today we live in a world that is more than 50 percent urban, and a substantial percentage of this population is living in informal settlements (UN-Habitat 2016). It is anticipated that this population will double by 2050 as climate migrants will move to cities to survive climate catastrophe and loss of livelihood. Let me begin by saying, we have been talking about beautiful buildings and fabulous designs in the last day and a half; but we have not talked about where 20 to 50 percent of people who live in cities actually reside: the Global South (UN-Habitat 2016). In this part of the world, a significant amount of housing stock is designed, financed, and constructed by the people who live in it (Hardoy and Satterthwaite 2013). There are no state resources or subsidies, and all you brilliant architects and planners have nothing to do with them. I ask, "Where do these people feature in this discussion?" Yesterday, John [Schellnhuber] said, "Oh, we like to work with them, but we have to deal with all the people who are emitters." However, our process of confronting the climate crisis cannot be sequential, just as mitigation, adaptation, resilience, destruction, loss, and damage are not sequential, rather a continuum. Therefore, you have to deal with them together.

My colleagues and I began to work in Mumbai. We were a small group of professionals committed to working in partnership with social movements that focused on stopping forced eviction of informal settlements. Our work produced an interesting strategy wherein we found that women-centered, local community-driven [initiatives] aggregated at the city, subnational, and national levels produced transformation for poor communities who live incrementally in amazing townships. These were towns within cities that have been ignored and were previously outside the city. Then the city tried to evict them.

What we tried to do was to create conditions by which first-, second-, third-, and fourth-generation migrants were shown the contributions they make to the city and were thus able to reformulate their self-image and how they are connected to the city. In 1988 we began an Asian coalition of housing rights, and in 1996 we formed Shack Dwellers International, in which today we have 33 countries and around 300 cities working together. We operate locally, but we make noise globally, and this is what I am trying to do here, to make all of you consider the implications of what happens to Indigenous communities and rural communities who are pushed into cities out of desperation; think of the people Ana María [Durán Calisto] and [Edgar Pieterse] spoke about. They are a mixture; they produce a new form of cosmopolitanism in informal settlements and transform the way cities are understood.

What do [slum dwellers] face? They face nonexistent amenities and services. There is a paradox that the largest pipe carrying water to the city of Mumbai goes through Dharavi but did not provide water to the slum till 1984. How did the water come to the slums? The dwellers made holes in the mains and put in pipes to divert the water from the water pipe. Often disruptions are both positive and nega-

Fig. 17.1 City water mains running through Dharavi, Mumbai

Fig. 17.2 Mahila Milan leaders

tive; however, when you do not give people a choice for their voice, representation, and right to participate in solutions, they produce negative disruption.

[At Shack/Slum Dwellers International (SDI)], we see that people in all our cities are facing every single crisis, which we, until four years ago, thought were just deficits of development. But we have been dragged kicking and screaming into the climate space as the world faces this imminent danger of exceeding the planetary capacity to cope with carbon emissions. We are now seeing that every single reason why people emigrate has a fundamental climate backdrop. Well, for poor people, what cities do [and do not do] for them and what the climate does for them are the same: they destroy their habitat, their livelihood, and produce the same level of complete devastation, with no accountability for the loss of assets, the inability to recover from this situation, and the absence of any state or city support. In our women-centered transformation process, we look at poor women in every city, who formed the basis of the new knowledge negotiations we do internally.

People like me and many young professionals within Shack/Slum Dwellers International are with community women to help them understand how cities function, their rights and their entitlements; and together we, as affiliates and member federations, produce disaggregated household data to provide evidence to the city of what they require from the city. We go to the state if the city says it is not

Fig. 17.3 Know Your City, pavilion at the World Urban Forum (WUF)

their business. We go to the national government if the state says it is not their business. If the national government says no, we come to the global space. The idea is to create a citizenship entitlement advocacy process for this aggregated volume of people who we know are going to grow exponentially, as we have seen during COVID-19, when so many unidentified city migrants suddenly popped up in so many of our cities. Governments are still seeking to gather data to identify these invisible circular migrants who come and go from cities. This is what we look like when we go to most places. A bunch of us also came here to the Vatican when the Pope invited us to meet social movements. We collect data at the household level, and we use whatever open-source digital systems we can, but it is not digital first. It is hand-drawn, hand-numbered documents that get digitized, so every household knows exactly what they do and we collect different data types. That data has produced a campaign called Know Your City.[1]

SDI always challenges our mayors, *do you know every single slum in your city?* Most of them only know those that are politically useful for their voting base, [but] they do not know most of them, they do not know where their people live, they do not know anything. What we do is invite opinion makers. Often famous politicians and other individuals visit our settlements. We use that publicity to challenge them about the neglect of the informal urban poor. We do not think that one such visit will change the situation, but rather that these actions create confi-

Fig. 17.4 Know Your City, Nairobi

dence amongst communities to talk to anybody who is an opinion maker or a driver of change. What these actions do is change the conversation from *I am poor, I need help* to *I am entitled to this. This is the evidence I have. These are the solutions that we have. Are you going to support and assist us?*

SDI is a regular fixture at international events. We will be at the World Urban Forum, where we meet mayors, ministers, and global and local stakeholders to explore possible partnerships and possible ways to engage them and work locally and globally with them.

We equally invest in building consensus around how our network and its members can make changes themselves. An example is the funicular roofing tiles that women have begun to use instead of an RCC ceiling or roof. The women designed them, manufactured them, and laid out roofs with these tiles, or LADDIS as we call them. All the men in the community said it would not work. *What did the women do?* They made the men sit on top of it to demonstrate that this was new material we would use. We also brought women to design the kind of houses that worked for them. We were deeply upset with professionals, especially architects and architecture schools. Why don't you work with challenges of informality in your cities? We said, *okay, we will build our houses, we will do our design, we build designs, and we do this in every city*. Then we invited mayors and ministers to take these designs up and try to get the city norms and standards to accept these changes.

Among the most disruptive acts, we built a house in the United Nations Headquarters lobby. The UN staff told us nobody could go to the UN building on Sunday before the meetings because passes were not given out. But we managed to have our whole team carry all the materials and build the house model. Then we were told that the house could not be entered because it was not insured. The Secretary-General, Kofi Annan, went and sat inside the house. Nobody could stop him. We became well-known in the global space because it became a location where every delegation came and took a picture of themselves against this backdrop.

Fig. 17.5 Kofi Annan in model house, UN Headquarters, New York

Fig. 17.6 SDI model house in UN lobby, New York

Over time, this has become an informal practical pathway of engagement. Our first challenge is to make friends with our worst enemies, or those who ignore us but whom we need for what we seek to do. It started with mayors, architects, planners, scientists, and finance people, because everybody ignored us. After a period of time, some of our best friends are now people from these professions. What we find is that now that we have come into the climate space, we believe that everybody's life is moving from dealing with anticipated disaster to resilience and adaptation. It is a continuum for poor people. *How do all of us support them?* Philanthropic money is not enough, we do not want you to domesticate us with projects. Rather, I want to plead with you *to listen to our demands and expectations of you: make us your partner, fight with us. We want you to argue with us if our science and our technologies are wrong. We will listen. We know how to argue. We know how to give you evidence. But do not patronize or pity us, and we are certainly not passive beneficiaries of your charity. We will be the people who will make your cities sustainable. We are the social infrastructure that saved all of you during COVID-19. Unfortunately, all the elite sing songs when they are in trouble and forget all about it when the crisis is over.* Right now, on behalf of all the social movements and all the communities of disenfranchised people, I want to bring their voices to the race to resilience, of which I am an ambassador.

Many choices that you make affect the rest of the world. As our friend [Francis Kéré] said yesterday to all of you in the Global North and the elite of the Global South: You are amazing, but fantastic standards mess us up, because our planners and architects love everything you do. We copy everything you do, and everything you do wrong, we also do wrong. To change the architecture of real partnerships, for example, more people like me (rather larger than me), community leaders, should be sitting here with you in large numbers. You need to have the courage to make room for people to participate. My plea to everybody is, do not go the old way and say, *priority one, priority two*. We have to do everything together, and there are enough stakeholders and actors for this.

Thank you.

---

1 https://knowyourcity.tv/

References

Hardoy, Jorge E., and David Satterthwaite. 2013 (1989). *Squatter Citizen: Life in the Urban Third World.* London: Earthscan.

UN-Habitat. 2016. *Slum Almanac 2015–2016: Tracking Improvement in the Lives of Slum Dwellers*. Nairobi, Kenya: UN-Habitat.

⟶

18
emergency architecture

Shigeru Ban

Thank you. I am an architect. Actually, after practicing for 10 years, I was disappointed with my profession, because we mainly work for privileged people, who have power and money. Power and money are invisible. They hire us to make a monument to show off their power to the public. I am not saying that I do not want to make monuments, but I really wanted to work for society. Not only for privileged people, but also for people who have lost their houses by natural disasters.

Also, I recognized that earthquakes never kill people, but the collapse of buildings kills people, and that is our responsibility as architects. Actually, after big disasters like earthquakes, architects look for new projects. When cities are rebuilt, we get more projects. However, people suffer in poor living conditions, in temporary shelters and temporary houses, before cities are rebuilt. I thought to myself, this is our responsibility as architects, to improve the poor living conditions after the disaster. This is why I began working in disaster areas.

When I started my own practice, without any architectural experience, I started designing exhibitions. Figure 18.1 is the first exhibition I designed, in 1984, for my favorite architect from Finland,

Fig. 18.1 Alvar Aalto exhibition, 1984

Fig. 18.2 Paper Weekend House

Alvar Aalto. Alvar Aalto used a lot of timber, but I could not afford it at the time. So what I did was use recycled paper tubes, which were available in my studio. After we finished the printing paper, I kept them because I hate throwing those things away. I used a small-diameter tube for the ceiling, like the Alvar Aalto–designed Viipuri library, and a larger-diameter tube was used for the freestanding partition. Unexpectedly, I found that this material was stronger than I first thought. Therefore, I began testing the material in a laboratory and found they were strong enough to make a building.

Figure 18.2 is my weekend house, which is not used because I have no weekends. I had to get special permission from the government to build a permanent building with such unusual material. I built it in 1990 and it is still there. A few years later, I was asked by a contractor to make that big roof, which can be built by a carpenter without any steel. This is another structure for which I needed to get government permission as a permanent structure, which still exists.

I began using recyclable material in 1985, before people started talking about ecology and recycling. Finally, people started talking about the environment. Figure 18.3 shows Expo 2000 in Germany, in the city of Hanover. The main theme was environmental issues, and because I was the only architect who used recyclable material for building, I was chosen to design the government pavilion. This pavilion was made of recycled paper tubes, locally sourced in Germany. As a part of the contract, we asked the Expo organizers to collect and recycle all materials after the building was demolished. I did not want to use concrete. I just made a wooden box filled with sand instead of a concrete foundation. The connection was fabric tape. Normally, architects use a polyvinyl chloride (PVC) membrane, but PVC is not environmentally friendly. I made the membrane from waterproof and fire-protected paper.

As I mentioned, in 1984, I had become tired of my profession as an architect. [When later, in 1994,] I found photos from a refugee camp in a magazine, I was surprised to see that the refugee shelters made by the United Nations High Commissioner for Refugees (UNHCR) were so poor. People were freezing, because during the rainy season, these shelters were not good enough to keep them warm. I thought, without improvements to the shelter, not even medical care can help here. So I wrote a letter to the UNHCR in Geneva to improve the shelter, but there was no reply. I went to Geneva without an appointment and I was lucky to meet a German architect who was responsible for shelter construction. I showed him my idea for improving the shelter using paper tubes, and I was accepted as a consultant.

At the time, the UNHCR shelter program was causing deforestation in the vicinity of the camps, because they only provided refugees with plastic sheets; it was the refugees themselves who had to cut the trees to make a frame for their shelter using the UNHCR plastic sheet. The UNHCR had started supplying aluminum pipes for the construction, but the material was expensive locally, so many would sell it and cut down trees again. This is when I proposed using recycled paper. I worked with Vitra to make some prototypes. I also wanted to design a more comfortable shelter. However, because of UN [and host country arrangements], shelters could not be too

Fig. 18.3 Japan Pavilion, Expo 2000 Hannover (next page)

comfortable, to avoid becoming permanent. So I was given a budget of US$50 per unit.

In 1995, the city of Kobe suffered a massive earthquake. I read in the newspaper that there were Vietnamese refugees suffering after the disaster. That was the time when the Japanese government first allowed the refugees from Vietnam to live in Kobe. These refugees were predominantly Catholic and gathered at church. When I arrived there, there was no church. Everything was destroyed and burned after the earthquake. Therefore, I proposed to the priest that we have a temporary church made out of paper. He did not believe it was possible. He said, "How can we make the building out of paper after the fire?" But I did not give up. Instead, I commuted to Kobe every Sunday. I became acquainted with the Vietnamese refugees. Sometimes temperatures inside the tents would reach more than 40°C, while on rainy days the tents would become flooded. The government started making temporary housing, but Kobe is quite a dense city, and most of the temporary houses were built outside the city. These people had jobs in a particular area, in a particular factory; if they moved to the government temporary housing, they would lose their jobs, so they wanted to keep living in this park. However, Japanese neighbors tried to kick them out, as they were afraid that this park might become a slum.

Fig. 18.4 Paper Log House, Japan

Fig. 18.5 Paper Church, Japan

We had to provide something more comfortable, healthier, but also something that could be accepted by neighbors by making the structures look temporary. People never believed that the house could be built from paper, but we built it with students, with paper tube walls and roof, and the foundation made of beer crates. We put sandbags inside the beer crates as typhoon preparation, and people lived there for four years.

After we constructed the shelters, the priest trusted me to rebuild the church out of paper. Student volunteers built with us, just 10 meters by 50 meters, inside this oval shape that comes from my favorite church in Rome, designed by Bernini. The structure stood for 10 years, although it was used for less. It became a symbol of the city, hosting concerts, weddings, and movies; it transformed into an important community space for the city. Then, 10 years later, the city decided to rebuild and I was lucky to design it.

Fig. 18.6 Paper Log House, Turkey

We disassembled the Kobe church and sent it over to Puli, Taiwan, after an earthquake there. It became a church and community center, which became the permanent community center and church. It still exists there. Then I wondered, what is the definition of a temporary and a permanent

Fig. 18.7 Paper Log House, India

structure? As you know, in big cities, there are so many concrete buildings made by developers, bought by other developers, then they destroy them and build new ones. Even building in concrete can be temporary, as long as the building was made to make money. Even a building made of paper, if accepted, can be permanent.

In 2001, in Turkey, after an earthquake, I was invited to make temporary houses [Figure 18.6]. All the paper tubes and plastic beer crates were donated free by a local manufacturer. The children helped us to put the waste paper inside the paper tubes to make them more insulated.

Figure 18.7 is from Gujarat, India, in 2001. I was asked to make temporary houses after another earthquake. It was easy. Paper tubes can be bought anywhere in the world. The only thing I could not find in Gujarat was beer crates, because nobody drinks beer in the area. The local Indian architect proposed that I use red Coca-Cola crates, but I saw these as out of context. Therefore, we made a traditional mud floor and mud foundation. Some of the houses were used as houses, some as schools. I received a letter from my local architect in India, who sent me a photo and said that the structures still exist as a local clinic. After 20 years, they still love it and take care of it, and they still keep it as a local clinic.

This is in Sri Lanka, in a fishermen's village that was totally destroyed by the tsunami after the Sumatra earthquake. We went there to use locally available mud, cement, and brick to build 50 houses after the village was totally destroyed.

Fig. 18.8 Kirinda House, Sri Lanka

In 2008, in Chengdu, China, during the Beijing Olympics, this city was totally destroyed by an earthquake. Over 30,000 people were killed; many children died because the school was so poorly built. I started making temporary houses. The local authority did not want a foreigner to make the houses. However, I met the schoolmaster. She asked me to make a temporary classroom. I brought my Japanese students, from Keio University, to work with local Chinese students for five weeks. We built nine classrooms over 500 square meters, just the students using paper tubes and locally available wooden joints. The school still stands.

Fig. 18.9 Haulin Temporary School, China

In 2009, L'Aquila, Italy. The whole city was totally destroyed by an earthquake. At that time here, Mr. Berlusconi, former prime minister, wanted to bring the G8 summit[1] to a resort island, but because of the

earthquake he suddenly decided to bring the G8 summit to L'Aquila. I met the mayor. He wanted a temporary music hall, because the city is famous for music, but no concert hall was available after the earthquake. The mayor provided the land, and with the Japanese prime minister, we held a joint Italian-Japanese press conference, showing the model for the building. As a result of the success of the conference, I received €500,000 to build this temporary concert hall. The wall is made of sandbags and temporary scaffolding. To insulate for sound, we covered the structure with donated red curtains; the inside is made of paper tubes for acoustical reasons, and the pillars are made of paper tubes. It still stands.

Fig. 18.10 Cardboard Cathedral, New Zealand (previous page)

In 2010, I flew to the Dominican Republic. I worked with local students in Santo Domingo to bring paper tubes and plastic sheets to make temporary shelters.

In 2011, in northern Japan, we had an earthquake, flooding, a tsunami, and nuclear contamination. People were evacuated to a gymnasium, but there was no privacy. I think privacy is a basic human right. We started making the privacy partition with a paper tube with just a fabric curtain. We built over 2,000 units in three months. Then we built three-story temporary houses with shipping containers next door.

In 2011, Christchurch, New Zealand. I received an email, when I was busy working in Fukushima, from the Reverend Craig Dixon. He said that you must be the architect who can design a temporary church for free. I said, the free charges mean that the structure must be used for public services, not only religious services. I went there and analyzed an original section diagram program. Then I built a temporary cathedral with the paper tube locally available. The foundation is made of shipping containers, and this became the symbol of the city and a tourist destination. This is also now a permanent church.

In 2015, in the Philippines, their biggest beer company, San Miguel, did not want to donate the paper and beer crates. Finally, I had to use red Coca-Cola crates.

Fig. 18.11 Housing for the displaced, Ukraine

In 2016, Nepal, we built the house and schools with the wooden frame and rubber bricks.

This is my most recent project: making partitions for Ukrainian refugees, in neighboring countries. They get out of the first train station after the border, they get registered and go to the big gymnasium without any privacy. I work with my colleague from the New European Bauhaus, Hubert Trammer, a Polish architect, working with local students. He donated paper tubes and cartons.

Finally, this is Dubno, Ukraine [Figure 18.11]. We have not gone there, but we sent over the unit, and local Ukrainian architects built the partitions themselves. We continue working for Ukraine. This is the second phase, where I am proposing to rebuild an apartment block. Affordable housing with a new system of Styrofoam, foam core, just painted with fiberglass-reinforced plastic—it is a typical technology. This is very inexpensive, locally made in Ukraine, and also creating new employment opportunities. This is the second project we are now preparing in Poland and in Ukraine.

Thank you very much.

1 At the time, Russia was part of the group.

→

19

built-environment education in recon-structing ukraine

Olena Vozniak

Today I will speak about the CANactions platform and its role in education about the built environment and offer some examples of CANactions. *What is CANactions?* CANactions is a platform acting in the sphere of architecture and urbanism established in Kyiv in 2008. Our mission is to enhance the creation of places and communities where people love to live and work. For more than 15 years, CANactions has been implementing the world's best practices in the fields of architecture and urban development through a number of educational and urban projects. Our policies are openness and accessibility for the maximum number of people, not indifferent to urban development and architecture, seeking relevant knowledge and changing the cities and places around them.

At the moment, the CANactions platform includes the CANactions Festival, CANactions School, CANactions Publishing House, and CANactions Competition Program. *How do we work?* We build a network of engaged professionals in Ukraine and worldwide. We create synergies between stakeholders to improve their decision-making in urban and regional planning. We facilitate dialogue between Ukraine and the world in order to integrate Ukraine and support international contacts.

The CANactions School was born in 2015, at a difficult but unique moment in Ukraine's history. There was war in Donbas, a deep economic crisis, and increasing skepticism about the feasibility of real change in the political system that had shaped existing Ukrainian realities. At the same time, these factors triggered great social demand for principled reform of the existing relationship between citizens and other government authorities. This immediately led to the questions: Who are those change makers who could moderate the process of building new types of cities? What tools and approaches do they need to be able to successfully deal with the complexity of the current challenges? All these issues became the starting point for establishing

Fig. 19.1 CANactions Festival 2019

Fig. 19.2 CANactions students undertaking planning exercises

CANactions School as a research-oriented and practice-based lab with a strong focus on urbanism. CANactions School is now an independent, non-formal educational institution that is aimed at the exploration of Ukrainian cities in defined concepts and actions for human development on strategic, as well as tactical, levels.

Thus, the school's key principles are a disciplinary approach, project-based learning, teamwork, experimental learning, a strategic approach to urban design and spatial planning, and cooperation with a vast network of international experts and institutions. As an institution that is based in Ukraine and is interested in the positive development of the country, CANactions uses quite an unusual approach for post-Soviet education. This is not to ignore the existing reality, with all its urbanism, constraints, and challenges, but to explicitly choose to work with it, communicating with different actors and finding the relevant solution for particular cases.

This openness to real urban life provokes the creation of various ideas and proposals, from small interventions to strategic transformations, that are aimed at bringing tangible changes to Ukraine and its cities. Since its inception, CANactions has been oriented toward collaborating with the world's leading experts in architecture and urbanism, building professional bridges between Ukraine and the world, and achieving prominent results in urban development. While working on the idea between education and practice, CANactions School has collaborated with city administrations and communities of such Ukrainian cities as Kyiv, Mariupol, Chernivtsi, Kramatorsk, Poltava, and many others. We also work on cases and in collaboration with the city administrations of Amsterdam, Rotterdam, Zurich, and Helsinki.

I would like to talk a little about our recent educational program, from 2021. It is called Spatial Planning for Accessibility, Cooperation and Economic Sustainability (SPACES). We did it in partnership with the Herias Foundation from Romania and explored the topic of spatial planning in the context of decentralization reform in Ukraine. The SPACES program works with a group of neighboring Ukrainian *hromadas*[1] and focuses on coordination or joint actions to increase accessibility of services and economic growth in the territories. A multidisciplinary team of professionals experienced in spatial planning, together with the representatives of the local government of Ukrainian *hromadas* communities, developed a regional spatial development concept. It was a Common Actions Concept with several territorial *hromadas* located nearby, sharing a common landscape and culture and similar economic civilization. The Concept coordinates the development regardless of organizational boundaries.

However, when we wrote the document on *hromadas*, there was a question on how to implement all the things that had been written

Fig. 19.3 CANactions student Expo 2025 poster

in this document. That is why *hromadas* needed some action plans, for example, on how to do it in the future. Besides the concept, participants of the program developed a non-formal and alternative concept product, which is the EXPO Boykivshchyna 2025. It will be a series of exhibition conferences, public discussions, and festivals that will take place in the summer of 2025 on the territory of SPACES. The Expo will demonstrate to potential investors the successful projects implemented in the territory during the last five years, which involve residents and the discussion of the common future. It represents the vision of the region's development.

Before the war, *hromadas* had already started preparations for the Expo. Moreover, they agreed on this future development in the common action concept. It was the first time in Ukraine that five *hromadas* stayed united and made plans for common development for the next few years. We are now communicating with people from these *hromadas*, and they say that this plan helps them in their war conditions regardless of the *hromadas*'s situation, which is near the front line and in the western part of Ukraine.

This case is useful and indicative for the future development of Ukraine and Ukrainian cities. It is about joining forces, cooperating, searching for their identity, relying on their past experience and achievements, and understanding their own vocations. It is also about looking at formal things from a different perspective, finding nonstandard solutions instead of reacting to current change, and improvisation. This plan accurately reflects the nonlinear nature of any full-fledged project. All this clearly demonstrates CANactions's approach. For the usefulness of any project, we believe that it is necessary to constantly monitor what is happening and look from different perspectives. This is what determines sustainability. This is also one of the answers to the question of how to proceed further. What is important for the successful development of the country, region, or

Fig. 19.4 CANactions student working group

Fig. 19.5 CANactions office, January 2022

territory is to build each round of development on the previous experience.

Looking at 14 years of function and evolution of CANactions, we can safely say that it reflects how Ukraine and its society have been developing over these years. The year 2015 changed the people and the country, and now we see how people are fighting. We see how people are behaving now. Even in the quiet territories, people have changed. People are more convinced of their choices and their values than ever.

Now, in 2022, we are again experiencing a period of great change. It is now more necessary than ever to revise the old institutions, including classic education, in their ways of planning and designing, their ways of building, and the whole attitude and thinking of the issue of living. The informality of institutions like, for example, CANactions allows us to be stable and flexible, and to quickly respond to all the challenges and changes we have. This does not mean that we have forgotten to build each round on the development from the previous experience.

Fig. 19.6
CANactions office, after the February invasion

What about the future? I would be happy to say today that we have a big, inspiring, and amazing plan for the reconstruction of Ukraine. But I cannot. Figure 19.5 shows our office in January 2022. It seems to me like another reality now. This is how it looks now [Figure 19.6]. On February 24, I left Kyiv with my kids. Our branches are located in different parts of the world now and in different cities in Ukraine. We, as a Ukrainian institution, need to satisfy our basic needs and secure the roof over our heads. However, it is still not over. There is still a war in Ukraine, but we are not victims. We are brave people. We are warriors. We continue to work. We are volunteering. We are supporting Ukrainian cities. We work with them and try to satisfy their basic needs for safety by supplying them with some equipment, some ideas, and some humanitarian help.

As an institution, we are in the process of formulating the format and strategic reason for our activity. We are not in a rush. We follow the principle of one step at a time. We truly believe that the most important thing in CANactions is connections. Moreover, often these connections are more important than even what they connect. We are open to dialogue and ideas. Ukrainian cities are open to cooperation. We invite everyone at the state or organizational level to join us. We are sure that everything will be rebuilt, but we need time to reflect, analyze, and find support; to understand the real numbers and scale of the tragedy, destruction, and loss. What we truly believe is that it is the only way to create a better future for Ukraine. The world has started acting and reflecting, creating and fostering new connections, developing effective proposals, and establishing a responsible attitude toward the cities and places in which we live.

We know that the quality of life in cities is determined by the ability of people to unite, hear each other, and find things in common. We can go on the basis of common values and goals in the family, city, country, and world. It is crucial now. I think it is our common responsibility, because only together can we overcome all of these challenges. Thank you very much.

1 Basic unit of administrative division in Ukraine, similar to a municipality. It was established by the government of Ukraine on June 12, 2020.

acknowledgments

We extend a heartfelt thank-you to the Laudes Foundation for their financial support of the June 9–10, 2022, conference and publication production costs.

We are thankful to MOD21 (ERBUD Group) for their donation toward the open access license for this publication.

Thank you to all those who provided testimonials from the conference, which are herewith included; and to Andrew Goodhouse and Franziska Schreiber for their feedback on the preface to this book.

To Gitta Köllner, Potsdam Institute for Climate Impact Research, thank you for your scientific fact-checking support for Hans Joachim Schellnhuber's contribution.

We thank all the participants at the Reconstructing the Future for People and Planet conference: Joachim von Braun, PAS President; H.Em. Card. Peter K.A. Turkson, PAS Chancellor; Hans Joachim Schellnhuber, Bauhaus Earth, PAS Academician; Wael Al Awar, waiwai; Dieter Babiel, ERBUD S.A.; Shigeru Ban, Shigeru Ban Architects; Donald Brenninkmeijer, Laudes Foundation; Thomas Brenninkmeijer, COFRA Holding AG; Francesca Bria, Italian National Innovation Fund; Rolf Buch, Vonovia SE; Marlène de Saussure, Bauhaus Earth; Christopher (Cade) Diehm, New Design Congress; Sandrine Dixson-Declève, Club of Rome; James Drinkwater, Laudes Foundation; Ana María Durán Calisto, Yale University/Estudio A0; Archbishop Paul R. Gallagher, Secretariat of State, Vatican City; Andrea Gebhard, German Federal Chamber of Architects; Klara Geywitz, German Federal Minister for Housing, Urban Development and Building; Dariusz Grzeszczak, ERBUD S.A.; Vicente Guallart, Valldaura Labs; Jeremy Higginbotham, Send/Receive; Daniel Ibáñez, IAAC; Bjarke Ingels, BIG Bjarke Ingels Group; Nathalie Jean-Baptiste, Julius Baer Foundation; Leslie Johnston, Laudes Foundation; Diébédo Francis Kéré, Kéré Architecture; Nina Kovsted Helk, Realdania; Andreja Kutnar, InnoRenew CoE; Lesley Lokko, African Futures Institute; Elspeth MacRae, Global Bioeconomy Forum; Wanjira Mathai, WRI; Liz McKeon, IKEA Foundation; Giovanna Melandri, MAXXI; Klaus Mindrup, E3G; Philipp Misselwitz, Bauhaus Earth; Brigitte Mohn, Bertelsmann Stiftung; Alan Organschi, Bauhaus Earth; Marc Palahí, European Forest

Institute; Sheela Patel, SPARC; Inger Paus, Google; Edgar Pieterse, African Centre for Cities; Veerabhadran Ramanathan, PAS Academician; Vyjayanthi Rao, Yale University; Carlo Ratti, Massachusetts Institute of Technology; Ruth Reichstein, European Commission; Tony Rinaudo, World Vision; H.E. Msgr. Marcelo Sánchez Sorondo, Vatican City; Volker Schlöndorff; Monica Tanuhandaru, Environmental Bamboo Foundation; H.E. President Ursula von der Leyen, European Commission; Olena Vozniak, CANactions; Geoffrey West, Santa Fe Institute; Jacqueline West; Marc Weissgerber, Bauhaus Earth; Xu Tiantian, DnA_Design and Architecture; and Amanda Yates, Auckland University of Technology.

We extend our gratitude to the Pontifical Academy of Sciences team: Gabriella Clare Marino, Simonetta Ulisse, Aldo Cicinelli, Francesco Mancini, and Alessandra Petrillo; Commissario Eugenio Cavinato, from Gendarmeria at the Vatican, and Francesco Iaboni, from Vatican IT.

Thank you to all those who donated the use of their images to this project.

Finally, thank you to the conference team: Dr. Marlène de Saussure, Christiane Walter, Nicole Pastrik, Lion Verheyden, Johanna Westermann, Jeremy Higginbotham, and Annie Schneider.

→

conference testimonials

Wael Al Awar

The Rome conference was a remarkable moment. It offered a unique opportunity to listen to, learn from, and discuss with leading voices in architecture, science, and policy making on the climate crisis—the most urgent question we face today. As an architect based in Dubai, I have always believed that I have a responsibility to read the regional ecosystem closely and to develop a future vernacular that can offer alternative solutions for the way we build. This is the basic idea underpinning waiwai's work in the Gulf, in Japan, and beyond. In Rome, it was clear that these concerns are shared on a deep level, and that they can form the fiber of a global network for the transformation of the built environment.

Dieter Babiel

It was an honor, a pleasure, and an enrichment at the same time to be a participant in this first conference in the heart of the Vatican, with attendees from all over the world.

A lot of us presented already existing local or national solutions regarding a transformation to sustainable, healthy, and eco-friendly building materials.

A huge asset for the construction and building materials sector to transform, adapt, and contribute in the best possible way for our common future and planet.

We all are expecting an enormous boost coming out of this meaningful conference. We will go on with that essential topic.

But it's not only a commitment by the politicians and scientists (like Ursula von der Leyen, Klara Geywitz, or John Schellnhuber, who all were actively participating in this conference); it's mainly a task for the production and construction companies, who all have the opportunity to be among the first, the best, when it comes to reconstructing our planet and future.

Shigeru Ban

It was a wonderful opportunity to attend the conference Reconstructing the Future for People and Planet in the Vatican. It was my first experience of a conference with such diverse experts working for the reconstruction of the future of our earth, and I enjoyed listening to "inconvenient truths" of our planet.

I was also amazed by the network of Dr. Hans Joachim Schellnhuber in the organization of this meaningful conference.

Rolf Buch (translated from German)
Buildings cause around 40 percent of global greenhouse gas emissions. This makes it clear: the housing sector has a special responsibility for the energy transition. The biggest lever is the upgrading of the existing stock. Our housing must be modernized on a large scale in a climate-friendly and energy-efficient way. Especially in view of the rapidly rising energy prices, there is no alternative.

Sandrine Dixson-Declève
As we commemorate the 50th anniversary of the seminal report to the Club of Rome, *Limits to Growth*, let us remember that we no longer have 50 years to embrace a new economic paradigm. There is no "one size fits all" for economic systems change, but we must learn to grow within limits. Our newest Earth for All system dynamic modeling and findings shows us that it is feasible to redesign economic and social policies to put our societies on a pathway toward well-being for all within planetary boundaries. The Bauhaus Earth approach contributes to this vision and enables us to redesign our urban infrastructure for both resilience to future shocks and stresses and a thriving well-being society.

Dariusz Grzeszczak (translated from German)
It was a great honor for me to be able to participate in such an interesting event with such strong content. I have to admit that I was a bit apprehensive at the beginning; not only do I represent Poland, which, euphemistically speaking, is not exactly a world leader in terms of ecology and certainly does not set any trends in the field of "sustainability," but I am also a representative of the construction industry. And this is not exactly one of the "cleanest" industries, to say the least. Compared with the aviation industry, we produce many times more CO_2 emissions. While flying accounts for "only" 3 percent of the global CO_2 footprint, the construction industry accounts for about 40 percent of greenhouse gas, depending on what is included in the calculation.

I have to admit that my family and I live quite a comfortable life thanks to concrete. However, I am only able to do this because 32 years ago I was given the opportunity to build up the largest independent Polish construction company. Of course, the change of political system in Poland at that time and the economic and investment boom after joining the European Union also played a decisive role.

Today, however, just making money and building wherever and whatever you like is a thing of the past. That is why I felt so comfortable at the workshop Reconstructing the Future. Here I was among people who share the same values, who imagine a similar future for the world, and not only focus on economic development but also act in a socially responsible way.

I am glad that, in addition to very interesting speeches and presentations, we also had the opportunity to share our experiences and reflect on current problems and challenges. The mix of business, politics, science, and NGOs was very inspiring. Although all participants came from different corners of the world, we all agreed: building has to change and become more sustainable.

I returned to Poland not only charged with positive energy but above all convinced that the path taken by my ERBUD Group is the right one. We will continue to expand the strategic area of renewable energies and also further develop our new start-up MOD21, with its modular timber construction.

I believe that the future belongs to these technologies and that we can thus make a decisive contribution to sustainable construction.

I am very grateful for the invitation. It was a very enriching experience for me.

Nina Kovsted Helk

"Imagine you have a fever, your body temperature has risen about one degree, and your temperature is 38°C. You have to go to work and go about your normal life. You can do that. It's not particularly pleasant, but it doesn't stop you from fulfilling your obligations.

"Now imagine that your fever rises another one degree, now you have a body temperature of 39°C. You still have to go to work and attend to your obligations. You can do that, but you can't deliver what you used to and you can't go on for much longer.

"Now imagine you have a body temperature of 40°C, your temperature has risen by about 3°C. You can no longer go to work and you can't meet your obligations. This is exactly how our planet feels."

John Schellnhuber opened the conference in Rome with that story. A metaphor we can all feel and understand from our own bodies. A metaphor that makes very clear the need for action—and that action must be NOW.

Andreja Kutnar

Sustainable built environments are regenerative and inclusive spaces that minimize environmental impacts through decarbonization and lead to positive societal and economic impacts. Non-exhaustively, this includes design and use considering beauty and functionality, land and material use, user perspectives and co-creation; and low environmental impacts via circular principles (construction, maintenance, life-extending solutions, and decon-

Fig. 21.1 Reconstructing the Future for People and Planet, 2022, conference participants

struction for reuse). Finally, this contributes to the health and well-being of users both directly and indirectly. To advance the field, it is important to combine modern research fields with concepts of sustainability and sensible use of natural resources, especially wood.

Lesley Lokko
Having the opportunity to discuss some of the most pressing concerns of our time in the company of such great thinkers, policy makers, and activists was beyond compare. It's rare to leave a conference with more questions than answers, and a renewed sense of hope that answers can—and will—be found.

Elspeth MacRae
The conference was an interesting blend of perspectives and contained some very exciting experiences contributing to ways to consider the future of the planet and to ameliorate the damage humans have wrought. The blend of backgrounds among attendees and presenters was also stimulating and provoked interesting observations.

Wanjira Mathai
The conference in Rome was an important signal of the role of all leaders in safeguarding our common planet, particularly as it pertains to the built environment.

Klaus Mindrup
The climate crisis is the biggest threat to many people worldwide. But crises

are also always an opportunity for new solutions and innovations.

These are set in motion by people and ideas. That is why the Reconstructing the Future conference in Rome was so important.

People who would otherwise never have come together thought about and discussed how we can save the world and at the same time change it for the better.

It was an honor for me to be there and I hope that this will be the beginning of a successful collaboration.

We owe it to future generations and to those who are already suffering greatly from the climate crisis.

Brigitte Mohn

If we only knew of the insights that have been derived from our science around the world, and if we could collectively transform that worldwide knowledge into solutions, we would be much further along by now. Under the direction of the Pontifical Academy of Sciences, and with a focus on Reconstructing the Future for People and Planet, a unique mix of experts from around the world gathered for an in-depth discussion on how to find national and regional solutions to address the global problem of the built environment, which accounts for approximately 40 percent of global greenhouse gas emissions.

These two days made it clear to me again that we will only find solutions to these projects if we work across disciplines and feed our knowledge into international ecosystems that innovatively combine, finance, and scale the solutions of science, research, civil society, and the economy with government sponsors.

Only if we really want this transformation—and if we are willing to combine equity, access, and connectivity with sustainability—will we find new paths that support life in community.

Veerabhadran Ramanathan

The focus on reducing emissions from the built environment is both pioneering and essential to bend the global warming curve. The conference managed to assemble an impressive group of thought leaders working on this topic who were willing to dive into the transdisciplinary aspects of the issue of the built environment.

Tony Rinaudo

What I sensed was that there was a lot of positive energy in the room and that highly motivated individuals were reporting on their extraordinary work of making the world a better place, especially in the built environment. The solutions were largely sustainable, nature friendly, and often mimicked nature, and always, because of this, gave an impression of wholesomeness and healthy, responsible living. The sessions gave a strong message of hope and reassurance that the solutions are at hand—we only need the will to implement them.

Volker Schlöndorff

To walk in the gardens of the Vatican, enjoying the sight of manicured plants and flowers, fine dining in a Renaissance palace built on the foundations of a former Roman palace built by Nero, meeting luminaries of the Accademia degli Cardinali—all these joys and privileges made it even more painful to follow the well-documented presentations of the dire state of a world threatened by climate change, overpopulation, and military conflicts.

The goodwill and commitment of the participants, the perfection of PowerPoint, video, and musical input, stood in sharp contrast to the indifference of governments and institutions more preoccupied with their own bureaucratic dysfunction than with the urgency of change.

All the measures necessary to be taken are known, all the solutions have been found, all the talking has been done—why is it so difficult to start acting on a larger scale?

From the little experience I have through my work with Tony Rinaudo, the "forest maker," I can only speak of one sector: agriculture in Africa. In the dry zone of the Sahel most afflicted by global warming, to achieve food security, priority should be given to:

1. Spread FMNR, *kisiki hai*, and *zaï* methods by multiple agents such as champion farmers. Minimize till and chemical fertilizers.
2. Develop cultivation of indigenous crops such as millet, cassava, et cetera, rather than import corn and wheat (from Ukraine).
3. Mechanization with small tractors and handheld motorized tools as used by smallholders in Asia.
4. Electrification by solar power plants with small-scale grids.

To be implemented by NGOs rather than governments, including the farmers themselves from the beginning. No planning from above, no big government development; no plans similar to the former five-year plans of socialism that utterly failed; avoiding administrations, bureaucracies, and corruption by working with other entities than the official ones.

A question came haunting me more and more as we talked and analyzed the situation, namely, when will humankind react as a species rather than as individuals or collectivities?

Geoffrey West

The conference on Reconstructing the Future for People and Planet, held in June at the Vatican in Rome, sponsored jointly by the Pontifical Academy of Sciences and Bauhaus Earth, was not just very timely but filled a crucial vacuum that has been absent from the many discussions concerning global sustainability. I am extremely grateful to the organizers for including me in this important and seminal conference.

We are surely facing the biggest challenge humans have yet confronted since evolving from being hunter-gatherers, with the very future of socioeconomic human society lying in the balance. This meeting convened a broad group of distinguished scientists, practitioners, politicians, religious leaders, and others for an intense two days of focusing on many of the practical challenges and potential solutions in dialogue with the big conceptual questions, such as growth, inequality, the North–South divide, et cetera. I very much enjoyed the eclectic nature of the gathering, the broad range of talks and perspectives, and the dedication to address the biggest challenge humans have yet faced. Bringing together a multidisciplinary group of thinkers focused on a major issue or scientific problem—any "complex adaptive system," for that matter—is what the Santa Fe Institute pioneered and is all about, so I'm very familiar with such gatherings. But what made this different and so pertinent and important was having a sizable number of practitioners and policy makers (and, in particular, politicians with influence) present—an obviously crucial ingredient if this is to ultimately have impact.

This was an excellent beginning and I hope you continue to push vigorously ahead with similar meetings, digging deeper into the specifics on the one hand, while exploring the bigger conceptual framework on the other. And I hope you keep me in mind for such future meetings!

Xu Tiantian

Many of the environmental and social challenges a developing country confronts have to do with disparate growth between urban and rural regions. As the labor force migrates to urban centers, the population in rural villages diminishes, often causing economic decline.

In the rural context, architecture has never been a stand-alone entity, but is intimately connected to its natural environment, local history and culture, the people, and their community, and in most situations it continues to be instrumental to providing solutions and possibilities for our current issues and challenges.

Integrative architecture that introduces social and economic measures may offer effective strategies for reviving rural villages. In fact, over the centuries, unique rural histories and traditions have nurtured and inspired social production. Today, reusing and adapting existing spatial resources is regarded around the world as an essential contribution to sustainable development. Reevaluating local resources and rediscovering Indigenous values are pressing and urgent challenges, yet they may provide new opportunities to rural regions. These conditions demand that architects expand their perspective in identifying issues and initiating collaborations.

The saying "Rural is global" should be adopted systematically, as local-scale interventions offer strategic and sustainable solutions. With many agrarian societies worldwide having practiced a way of life based on notions of balancing harmony between humans and nature, the rural continues to be a timeless model from which contemporary architects can draw wisdom.

index

MASTERPIECE
OF VENETIAN
San Rocco
Catalonia
in Venice
17. Mostra
Internazionale
di Architettura
Eventi Collaterali
La Biennale di Venezia
air
National Pavilion UAE
Wael Al Awar
Kenichi Teramoto
أرضٌ لَدِنَة
WETLAND
National Pavilion United Arab Emirates
ARSENALE – SALE D'ARMI VENICE, ITALY
Partecipazioni Nazionali
MAAR
in collaborazione
in collaboration w

Arte
Architettura
Cinema
Danza
Musica
Teatro
Archivio Storico
ALE
TTURA
21.11
ZIA
RSENALE
Free entry.
ROLEX
ether?
ROLEX

image credits

pp. 6/7 © DnA / Wang Ziling

pp. 12–15 © Gabriella Clare Marino/PAS

pp. 16/17 Courtesy of Sheela Patel

Fig. 2.1 © Hans Joachim Schellnhuber & Rick Lehmans

Fig. 2.2 © IPCC 2018

Fig. 2.3 © Rosa Hanhausen/Bauhaus Earth

Fig. 4.1, Fig. 4.2 © InnoRenew CoE

Fig. 4.3 G. C. Vittori, 1777 from Panjek, Aleksander. 2015. *Kulturna krajina in okolje Krasa: o rabi naravnih virov v novem veku.* Koper, Slovenia: Založba Univerze na Primorskem, www.hippocampus.si/ISBN/978-961-6963-35-0.pdf

Fig. 4.4, Fig. 4.5 © Eva Prelovšek Niemela

Figs. 5.1–5.13 © DnA/Wang Ziling

Fig. 5.14 © DnA/Fan Wenyun

Fig. 6.1 Courtesy of Ana María Durán Calisto

Fig. 6.2, Fig. 6.3 © Sistema Nacional de Información de Tierras Rurales e Infraestructura Tecnológica (SIGTIERRAS), Ecuador

Fig. 6.4, Fig. 6.5 Courtesy of Ana María Durán Calisto

Fig. 6.6, Fig. 6.7 © Taku Samejima

Fig. 7.1 © iStock

Fig. 7.2 © Wael Al Awar

Fig. 7.3 © Farah Al Qasimi, Sabkha, Al Ruwais, 2020, Courtesy of National Pavilion UAE, La Biennale di Venezia

Figs. 7.4–7.6 Courtesy of National Pavilion UAE, La Biennale di Venezia, and waiwai

Fig. 7.7, Fig. 7.8 © Muga Miyahara, Courtesy of National Pavilion UAE, La Biennale di Venezia, and waiwai

Fig. 7.9 © Farah Al Qasimi, Courtesy of National Pavilion UAE, La Biennale di Venezia, and waiwai

Fig. 7.10 Courtesy of National Pavilion UAE, La Biennale di Venezia, and waiwai

Fig. 7.11 © Frederico Torra, Courtesy of National Pavilion UAE, La Biennale di Venezia, and waiwai

Fig. 8.1 © Ajuntament de Barcelona

Fig. 8.2 © Ajuntament de Barcelona/Lamberto Ramon Torres

Fig. 8.3 © Ajuntament de Barcelona/Mariona Gil

Fig. 8.4 © Ajuntament de Barcelona/Curro Palacios

Fig. 9.1, Fig. 9.2 © World Inequality Report 2022

Fig. 9.3, Fig. 9.4 © Kounkuey Design Initiative (KDI)

Figs. 10.1–10.10 Courtesy of Geoffrey West; Fig. 10.8 Steffen, Will, Wendy Broadgate, Lisa Deutsch, Owen Gaffney, and Cornelia Ludwig. 2015. "The Trajectory of the Anthropocene: The Great Acceleration." *Anthropocene Review* 2, no. 1, 81–98, https://journals.sagepub.com/doi.org/10.1177/2053019614564785

Fig. 11.1, Fig. 11.2 © B & O Group

Fig. 11.3 © Christian Frey

Fig. 13.1 Steffen, Will, Katherine Richardson, Johan Rockström, Sarah E. Cornell, Ingo Fetzer, Elena M. Bennett, Reinette Biggs, et al. 2015. "Planetary Boundaries: Guiding Human Development on a Changing Planet." *Science* 347, no. 6223 (January 15), www.science.org/doi/10.1126/science.1259855

Fig. 13.2, Fig. 13.3 Provided by Scion, © David Trubridge Design

Fig. 13.4 © Scion

Fig. 13.5 © MELiSSA Foundation

Fig. 13.6, Fig. 13.7 © Clouds AO/SEArch

Fig. 14.1, Fig. 14.2 Pauleit, S., T. Zölch, and J. Brasche. 2018. "Grüne Infrastruktur für resiliente Städte." *Anthos* 3/18

Fig. 15.1 Kubiszewski, Ida, Robert Costanza, Carol Franco, Philip Lawn, John Talberth, Tim Jackson, and Camille Aylmer. 2013. "Beyond GDP: Measuring and Achieving Global Genuine Progress." *Ecological Economics* 93 (September): 57–68, https://doi .org/10.1016/j.ecolecon.2013.04.019

Fig. 15.2 © FAO

Fig. 15.3 © Marc Palahí

Fig. 16.1 © Pedro M. Cruz

Fig. 16.2, Fig. 16.3 CRA—Carlo Ratti Associati

Figs. 17.1–17.6 Courtesy of Sheela Patel

Fig. 18.1 © Shimizu Yukio

Fig. 18.2, Fig. 18.3 © Hiroyuki Hirai

Fig. 18.4 © Takanobu Sakuma

Fig. 18.5 © Hiroyuki Hirai

Fig. 18.6 © Shigeru Ban Architects

Fig. 18.7 © Kartikeya Shodhan

Fig. 18.8 © Eresh Weerasuriya

Fig. 18.9 © Lin Ju

Fig. 18.10 © Stephen Goodenough

Fig. 18.11 © Shigeru Ban Architects

Figs. 19.1–19.6 © CANactions

pp. 222/223 © Shigeru Ban Architects

Fig. 21.1 © Gabriella Clare Marino/PAS

pp. 238/239 © Frederico Torra, Courtesy of National Pavilion UAE, La Biennale di Venezia

notes

notes

notes

imprint

Bauhaus Earth, Hans Joachim Schellnhuber,
Rocío Armillas Tiseyra (Eds.)

Content and Production Secondary: Lion Verheyden

Contributing Authors: Wael Al Awar, Rocío Armillas Tiseyra, Shigeru Ban, Francesca Bria, Sandrine Dixson-Declève, Ana María Durán Calisto, Andrea Gebhard, Andreja Kutnar, Elspeth MacRae, Giovanna Melandri, Klaus Mindrup, Fredric Mosley, Marc Palahí, Sheela Patel, Edgar Pieterse, Carlo Ratti, Hans Joachim Schellnhuber, Joachim von Braun, Ursula von der Leyen, Olena Vozniak, Venla Wallius, Geoffrey West, and Xu Tiantian

Bauhaus Earth at Rechenzentrum,
Dorfstraße 46, 14467 Potsdam, Germany

Bauhaus Earth Lab, Im Marienpark 16,
12107 Berlin, Germany

https://www.bauhauserde.org
contact@bauhauserde.org

Printed with the financial support of Laudes Foundation

Acquisitions Editor:
David Marold, Birkhäuser Verlag, Vienna, Austria

Content and Production Editor:
Katharina Holas, Birkhäuser Verlag, Vienna, Austria

Copyediting / Proofreading:
John Sweet, Montréal, Canada

Layout, cover design, and typography:
Kathleen Bernsdorf, Berlin, Germany

Image editing:
Pixelstorm Litho & Digital Imaging, Vienna, Austria

Printing:
Holzhausen, die Buchmarke der
Gerin Druck GmbH, Wolkersdorf, Austria

Paper:
Nautilus Classic 120 g/m², Remake Smoke 380 g/m²

Library of Congress Control Number: 2022949049

Bibliographic information published by the German National Library

The German National Library lists this publication in the Deutsche Nationalbibliografie; detailed bibliographic data are available on the Internet at http://dnb.dnb.de.

Open Access License financial support given by MOD21 (ERBUD Group)

ISBN 978-3-0356-2697-1
e-ISBN (PDF) 978-3-0356-2701-5 Open Access
DOI: https://doi.org/10.1515/9783035627015

The book is published open access at www.degruyter.com.

How to cite this work:
Bauhaus Earth, Schellnhuber, H. J. & Armillas Tiseyra, R. (eds.). 2023. Reconstructing the Future: Cities as Carbon Sinks. Birkhäuser: Basel.

9 8 7 6 5 4 3 2 1 www.birkhauser.com

FSC www.fsc.org MIX Papier aus verantwortungsvollen Quellen FSC® C108696